glencoe
teen**health**
tobacco, alcohol + other drugs

McGraw
Graw
Hill

Bothell, WA • Chicago, IL • Columbus, OH • New York, NY

Meet the Authors

Mary H. Bronson, Ph.D. recently retired after teaching for 30 years in Texas public schools Bronson taught health education in grades K–12 as well as health education methods classes graduate and undergraduate levels. As Health Education Specialist for the Dallas School Distr Bronson developed and implemented a district-wide health eduation program. She has been hon as Texas Health Educator of the Year by the Texas Association for Health, Physical Education, Re and Dance and selected Teacher of the Year twice by her colleagues. Dr. Bronson has assisted districts throughout the country in developing local health education programs. She is also coauthor of Glencoe Health

Michael J. Cleary, Ed.D., C.H.E.S. is a professor at Slippery Rock University, where he teac methods courses and supervises field experiences. Dr. Cleary taught health education at Eva Township High School in Illinois and later served as the Lead Teacher Specialist at the Mc Center for Health Education in Fort Wayne, Indiana. Dr. Cleary has published widely on curri development and assessment in K–12 and college health education. Dr. Cleary is also coau Glencoe Health

Betty M. Hubbard, Ed.D., C.H.E.S. has taught science and health education in grades 6– as well as undergraduate- and graduate-level courses. She is a professor at the University of C Arkansas, where in addition to teaching she conducts in-service training for health education teac in school districts throughout Arkansas. In 1991, Dr. Hubbard received the university's tea excellence award. Her publications, grants, and presentations focus on research-based, compreh health instruction. Dr. Hubbard is a fellow of the American Association for Health Education and s as the contributing editor of the Teaching Ideas feature of the American Journal of Health Educ

Contributing Author

Dinah Zike, M.Ed. is an international curriculum consultant and inventor who has designed a developed educational products and three-dimensional, interactive graphic organizers for more t 35 years. As president and founder of Dinah-Might Adventures, L.P., Dinah is author of more tha award-winning educational publications. Dinah has a B.S. and an M.S. in educational curriculum instruction from Texas A&M University. Dinah Zike's Foldables® are an exclusive feature of McG

MHEonline.com

Copyright © 2014 by McGraw-Hill Education

Send all inquiries to:
McGraw-Hill Education
STEM Learning Solutions Center
8787 Orion Place
Columbus, OH 43240

ISBN: 978-0-07-664046-1
MHID: 0-07-664046-9

Printed in the United States of America.

8 9 10 11 12 LMN 23 22 21 20

STEM McGraw-Hill is committed to providing instructional materials in Science, Technology, Engineering, and Mathematics (STEM) that give all students a solid foundation, one that prepares them for college and careers in the 21st century.

Reviewers

Professional Reviewers

Amy Eyler, Ph.D., CHES
Washington University in St. Louis
St. Louis, Missouri

Shonali Saha, M.D.
Johns Hopkins School of Medicine
Baltimore, Maryland

Roberta Duyff
Duyff & Associates
St. Louis, MO

Teacher Reviewers

Lou Ann Donlan
Altoona Area School District
Altoona, PA

Steve Federman
Loveland Intermediate School
Loveland, Ohio

Rick R. Gough
Ashland Middle School
Ashland, Ohio

Jacob Graham
Oblock Junior High
Plum, Pennsylvania

William T. Gunther
Clarkston Community Schools
Clarkston, MI

Ellie Hancock
Somerset Area School District
Somerset, PA

Diane Hursky
Independence Middle School
Bethel Park, PA

Veronique Javier
Thomas Cardoza Middle School
Jackson, Mississippi

Patricia A. Landon
Patrick F. Healy Middle School
East Orange, NJ

Elizabeth Potash
Council Rock High School South
Holland, PA

The Path to Good Health

Your health book has many features that will aid you in your learning. Some of these features are listed below. You can use the map at the right to help you find these and other special features in the book.

* The **Big Idea** can be found at the start of each lesson.

* Your **Foldables®** help you organize your notes.

* The **Quick Write** at the start of each lesson will help you think about the topic and give you an opportunity to write about it in your journal.

* The **Bilingual Glossary** contains vocabulary terms and definitions in Spanish and English.

* **Health Skills Activities** help you learn more about each of the 10 health skills.

* **Infographs** provide a colorful, visual way to learn about current health news and trends.

* The **Fitness Zone** provides an online fitness resource that includes podcasts, videos, activity cards, and more!

* **Hands-On Health Activities** give you the opportunity to complete hands-on projects.

* **Videos** encourage you to explore real life health topics.

* **Audio** directs you to online audio chapter summaries.

* **Web Quest** activities challenge you to relate lesson concepts to current health news and research.

* **Review** your understanding of health concepts with lesson reviews and quizzes.

What's the word on the street? The **glossary** lists vocabulary terms in English and Spanish.

Quick! Write about your good health habits using a **Quick Write** activity.

Think big! Start your journey with a **Big Idea** and increase your pace with **Foldables®**.

Sharpen your skills with **Health Skills Activities**.

Got a nose for news? Check out each chapter's **infographs** for health news and trends.

Get into the zone –the **Fitness Zone!** Listen to podcasts, watch videos, and more.

Show what you know by completing a **Hands-On Health Activity**.

Stop! Look and Listen! Watch a Health eSpotlight **video** and explore real life health topics. Listen to the **audio** summaries to review the chapter.

Go on a quest. Take a **Web Quest** to learn more about health news and research.

Finish strong! **Review** your understanding of health concepts with lesson reviews and quizzes.

Contents

F4F-1 through F4F-9
Flip your book over to see a special section on fitness.

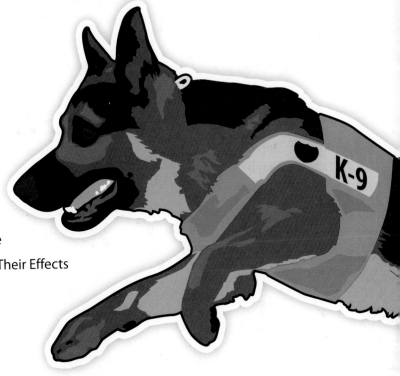

chapter 4 Using Medicines Wisely

Your Total Health

WHAT IS HEALTH?

Do you know someone you would describe as "healthy"? What kinds of traits do they have? Maybe they are involved in sports. Maybe they just "look" healthy. Looking fit and feeling well are important, but there is more to having good health. Good health also includes getting along well with others and feeling good about yourself.

Your **physical**, **emotional**, and **social** *health* are all **related** and make up your *total* **health.**

Health, the *combination of physical, mental/emotional, and social well-being,* may look like the sides of a triangle. You need all three sides to make the triangle. Each side supports the other two sides. Your physical health, mental/emotional health, and social health are all related and make up your total health.

Physical Health

Physical health is one side of the health triangle. Engaging in physical activity every day will help to build and maintain your physical health. Some of the ways you can improve your physical health include the following:

- ❀ **EATING HEALTHY FOODS** Choose nutritious meals and snacks.

- ❀ **VISITING THE DOCTOR REGULARLY** Get regular checkups from a doctor and a dentist.

- ❀ **CARING FOR PERSONAL HYGIENE** Shower or bathe each day. Brush and floss your teeth at least twice every day.

- ❀ **WEARING PROTECTIVE GEAR** When playing sports, using protective gear and following safety rules will help you avoid injuries.

- ❀ **GET ENOUGH SLEEP** Most teens need about nine hours of sleep every night.

You can also have good physical health by avoiding harmful behaviors, such as using alcohol, tobacco, and other drugs. The use of tobacco has been linked to many diseases, such as heart disease and cancer.

Mental/Emotional Health

Another side of the health triangle is your mental/emotional health. How do you handle your feelings, thoughts, and emotions each day? You can improve your mental/emotional health by talking and thinking about yourself in a healthful way. Share your thoughts and feelings with your family, a trusted adult, or with a friend.

If you are mentally and emotionally healthy, you can face challenges in a positive way. Be patient with yourself when you try to learn new subjects or new skills. Remember that everybody makes mistakes—including you! Next time you can do better.

Taking action to reach your goals is another way to develop good mental/emotional health. This can help you focus your energy and give you a sense of accomplishment. Make healthful choices, keep your promises, and take responsibility for what you do, and you will feel good about yourself and your life.

Social Health

A third side of the health triangle is your social health. Social health means how you relate to people at home, at school, and everywhere in your world. Strong friendships and family relationships are signs of good social health.

Do you get along well with your friends, classmates, and teachers? Do you spend time with your family? You can develop skills for having good relationships. Good social health includes supporting the people you care about. It also includes communicating with, respecting, and valuing people. Sometimes you may disagree with others. You can disagree and express your thoughts, but be thoughtful and choose your words carefully.

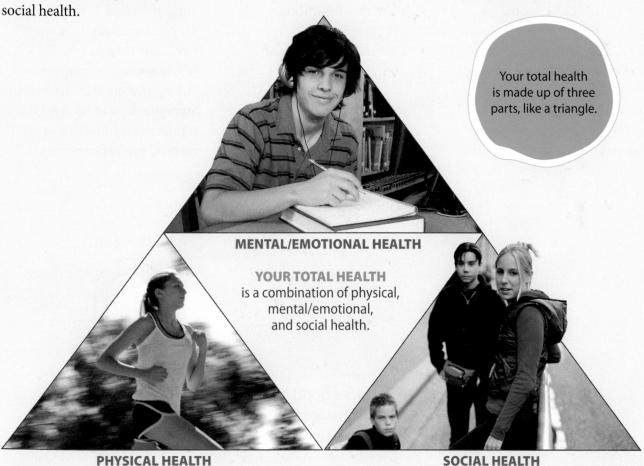

Your total health is made up of three parts, like a triangle.

MENTAL/EMOTIONAL HEALTH

YOUR TOTAL HEALTH is a combination of physical, mental/emotional, and social health.

PHYSICAL HEALTH

SOCIAL HEALTH

ACHIEVING WELLNESS

What is the difference between health and wellness? Wellness *is a state of well-being or balanced health over a long period of time.* Your health changes from day to day. One day you may feel tired if you did not get enough sleep. Maybe you worked very hard at sports practice. The next day, you might feel well rested and full of energy because you rested. Your emotions also change. You might feel sad one day but happy the next day.

Your overall health is like a snapshot of your physical, mental/emotional, and social health. Your wellness takes a longer view. Being healthy means balancing the three sides of your health triangle over weeks or months. Wellness is sometimes represented by a continuum, or scale, that gives a picture of your health at a certain time. It may also tell you how well you are taking care of yourself.

The Mind-Body Connection

Your emotions have a lot to do with your physical health. Think about an event in your own life that made you feel sad. How did you deal with this emotion? Sometimes people have a difficult time dealing with their emotions. This can have a negative effect on their physical health. For example, they might get headaches, backaches, upset stomachs, colds, the flu, or even more serious diseases. Why do you think this happens?

Your mind and body connect through your nervous system. This system includes thousands of miles of nerves. The nerves link your brain to your body. Upsetting thoughts and feelings sometimes affect the signals from your brain to other parts of your body.

Your **emotions** have *a lot* to do with *your* **physical health.**

The mind-body connection describes *how your emotions affect your physical and overall health and how your overall health affects your emotions.* This connection shows again how important it is to keep the three sides of the health triangle balanced. If you become very sad or angry, or if you have other strong emotions, talk to someone. Sometimes talking to a good friend helps. Sometimes you may need the services of a counselor or a medical professional.

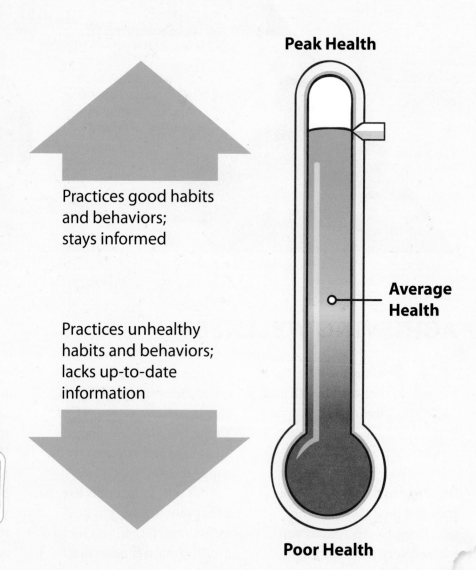

Practices good habits and behaviors; stays informed

Practices unhealthy habits and behaviors; lacks up-to-date information

The Wellness Scale identifies how healthy you are at a given point in time.

Peak Health

Average Health

Poor Health

Health Influences *and* Risk Factors

WHAT INFLUENCES YOUR HEALTH?

What are your favorite foods or activities? Your answers reflect your personal tastes, or likes and dislikes. Your health is influenced by your personal tastes and by many other factors such as:

- heredity
- environment
- family and friends
- culture
- media
- attitudes
- behavior

Heredity

You can control some of these factors, but not all of them. For example, you cannot control the natural color of your hair or eyes. **Heredity** (huh•RED•i•tee) is *the passing of traits from parents to their biological children.* Heredity determines the color of your eyes and hair, and other physical traits, or parts of your appearance. Genes are the basic units of heredity. They are made from chemicals called DNA, and they create the pattern for your physical traits. You inherited, or received, half of your DNA from your mother and half from your father.

Traits such as eye and hair color are inherited from parents.

Environment

Think about where you live. Do you live in a city, a suburb, a small town, or in a rural area? Where you live is the physical part of your **environment** (en•VY•ruhn•mehnt), or *all the living and nonliving things around you.*

Environment is another factor that affects your personal health. Your physical environment includes the home you live in, the school you attend, and the air and water around you.

Your *social environment* includes the people in your life. They can be friends, classmates, and neighbors. Your friends and **peers,** or *people close to you in age who are a lot like you,* may influence your choices.

You may feel pressure to think and act like them. Peer pressure can also influence health choices. The influence can be positive or negative. Helping a friend with homework, volunteering with a friend, or simply listening to a friend are examples of positive peer influence. A friend who wants you to drink alcohol, for example, is a negative influence. Recreation is also a part of your social environment. Playing games and enjoying physical activities with others can have a positive effect on your health.

©Jenny Elia Pfeiffer/Corbis

Culture

Your family is one of the biggest influences on your life. It shapes your cultural background, or *the beliefs, customs, and traditions of a specific group of people.* You learned that your family influences your health. In addition to your family, your culture, or *the collected beliefs, customs, and behaviors of a group,* also affects your health. Your family and their culture may influence the foods you eat as well as the activities and special events you celebrate with special foods. Some families fast (do not eat food) during religious events. Ahmed's family observes the holiday of Ramadan.

During this holiday, members of his family fast until sundown. Your family might also celebrate traditions that include dances, foods, ceremonies, songs, and games. Your culture can also affect your health. Knowing how your lifestyle and family history relate to health problems can help you stay well.

Media

What do television, radio, movies, magazines, newspapers, books, billboards, and the Internet have in common? They are all forms of media, or *various methods for communicating information.* The media is another factor that affects your personal health.

The media provide powerful sources of information and influence.

You may learn helpful new facts about health on the Internet or television. You might also see a commercial for the latest video game or athletic shoes. The goal of commercials on television or the Internet, as well as advertisements in print, is to make you want to buy a product. The product may be good or bad for your health. You can make wise health choices by learning to evaluate, or *determine the quality* of everything you see, hear, or read.

The celebration of Kwanzaa is a tradition in many African American families.

YOUR BEHAVIOR AND YOUR HEALTH

Do you protect your skin from the sun? Do you get enough sleep so that you are not tired during the day? Do you eat healthful foods? Do you listen to a friend who needs to talk about a problem? Your answers to these questions reflect your personal lifestyle factors, or *the behaviors and habits that help determine a person's level of health.* Positive lifestyle factors promote good health. Negative lifestyle factors promote poor health.

Positive lifestyle factors promote **good** health.

Your attitude, or your *feelings and beliefs,* toward your personal lifestyle factors plays an important role in your health. You will also have greater success in managing your health if you keep a positive attitude. Teens who have a positive attitude about their health are more likely to practice good health habits and take responsibility for their health.

Risk Behaviors

"Dangerous intersection. Proceed with caution." "Don't walk." "No lifeguard on duty." You have probably seen these signs or similar signs. They are posted to warn you about possible risks or dangers and to keep you safe.

Eating well-balanced meals, starting with a good breakfast.

Getting at least 60 minutes of physical activity daily.

Sleeping at least eight hours every night.

Doing your best in school and other activities.

Avoiding tobacco, alcohol, and other drugs.

Following safety rules and wearing protective gear.

Relating well to family, friends, and classmates.

Lifestyle factors affect your personal health.

Risk, or *the chance that something harmful may happen to your health and wellness,* is part of everyday life. Some risks are easy to identify. Everyday tasks such as preparing food with a knife or crossing a busy street both carry some risk. Other risks are more hidden. Some foods you like might be high in fat.

You cannot avoid every kind of risk. However, the risks you can avoid often involve risk behavior. A risk behavior is an action or behavior that might cause injury or harm to you or others. Playing a sport can be risky, but if you wear protective gear, you may avoid injury. Wear a helmet when you ride a bike to avoid the risk of a head injury if you fall. Smoking cigarettes is another risk behavior that you can avoid. Riding in a car without a safety belt is a risk behavior you can avoid by buckling up. Another risk behavior is having a lifestyle with little physical activity, such as sitting in front of the TV or a computer instead of being active. You can avoid many kinds of risk by taking responsibility for your personal health behaviors and avoiding risk.

RISKS AND CONSEQUENCES

All risk behaviors have consequences. Some consequences are minor or short-term. You might eat a sweet snack just before dinner so that you lose your appetite for a healthy meal. Other risk behaviors may have serious or life-threatening consequences. These are long-term consequences.

Experimenting with alcohol, tobacco, or other drugs has long-term consequences that can seriously damage your health. They can affect all three sides of your health triangle. They can lead to dangerous addictions, which are physical and mental dependencies.

These substances can confuse the user's judgment and can increase the risks he or she takes. Using these substances may also lead to problems with family and friends, and problems at school.

Risks that affect your health are more complicated when they are **cumulative risks** (KYOO•myuh•luh•tiv), which occur *when one risk factor adds to another to increase danger.* For example, making unhealthy food choices is one risk. Not getting regular physical activity is another risk. Add these two risks together over time, and you raise your risk of developing diseases such as heart disease and cancer.

Many choices you make affect your health. Knowing the consequences of your choices and behaviors can help you take responsibility for your health.

Reducing Risks

Practicing **prevention,** *taking steps to avoid something,* is the best way to deal with risks. For example, wear a helmet when you ride a bike to help prevent head injury. Slow down when walking or running on wet or icy pavement to help prevent a fall. Prevention also means watching out for possible dangers. When you know dangers are ahead, you can avoid them and prevent accidents.

Physical injury can be a consequence of risk behaviors.

ERproductions Ltd/Blend Images LLC

xiv

STAYING INFORMED You can take responsibility for your health by staying informed. Learn about developments in health to maintain your own health. Getting a physical exam at least once a year by a doctor is another way to stay informed about your health.

CHOOSING ABSTINENCE

If you practice abstinence from risk behaviors, you care for your own health and others' health by preventing illness and injury. Abstinence is *the conscious, active choice not to participate in high-risk behaviors.* By choosing not to use tobacco, you may avoid getting lung cancer. By staying away from alcohol, illegal drugs, and sexual activity, you avoid the negative consequences of these risk behaviors.

Abstinence is good for all sides of your health triangle. It promotes your physical health by helping you avoid injury and illness. It protects your mental/emotional health by giving you peace of mind. It also benefits your relationships with family members, peers, and friends. Practicing abstinence shows you are taking responsibility for your personal health behaviors and that you respect yourself and others. You can feel good about making positive health choices, which will strengthen your mental/emotional health as well as your social health.

- ☑ Plan ahead.
- ☑ Think about consequences.
- ☑ Resist negative pressure from others.
- ☑ Stay away from risk takers.
- ☑ Pay attention to what you are doing.
- ☑ Know your limits.
- ☑ Be aware of dangers.

Reducing risk behaviors will help maintain your overall health.

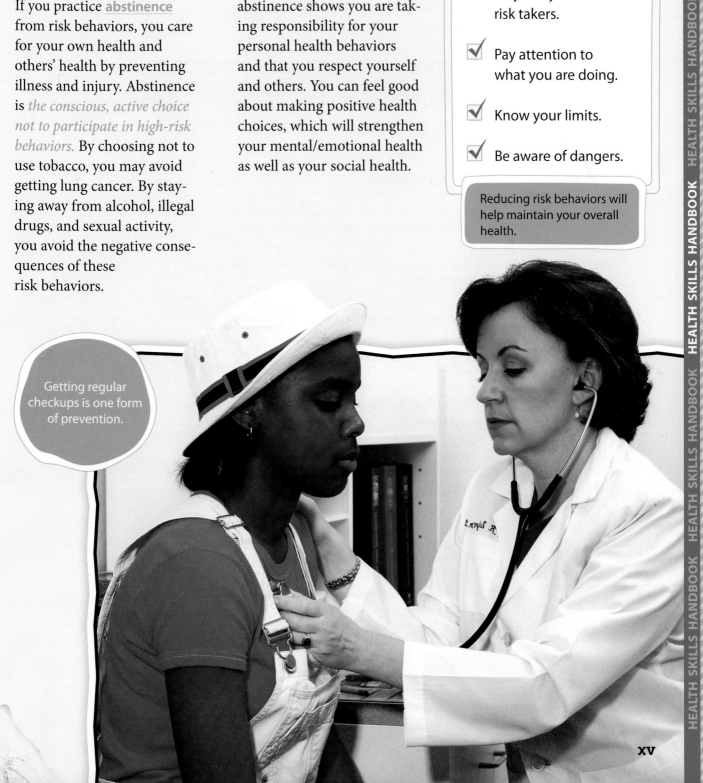

Getting regular checkups is one form of prevention.

Building Health Skills

SKILLS FOR A HEALTHY LIFE

Health skills are *skills that help you become and stay healthy.* Health skills can help you improve your physical, mental/emotional, and social health. Just as you learn math, reading, sports, and other kinds of skills, you can learn skills for taking care of your health now and for your entire life.

These ten skills affect your physical, mental/emotional, and social health and can benefit you throughout your life.

Health Skills	What It Means to You
Accessing Information	You know how to find valid and reliable health information and health-promoting products and services.
Practicing Healthful Behaviors	You take action to reduce risks and protect yourself against illness and injury.
Stress Management	You find healthy ways to reduce and manage stress in your life.
Analyzing Influences	You recognize the many factors that influence your health, including culture, media, and technology.
Communication Skills	You express your ideas and feelings and listen when others express theirs.
Refusal Skills	You can say no to risky behaviors.
Conflict-Resolution Skills	You can work out problems with others in healthful ways.
Decision Making	You think through problems and find healthy solutions.
Goal Setting	You plan for the future and work to make your plans come true.
Advocacy	You take a stand for the common good and make a difference in your home, school, and community.

SELF-MANAGEMENT SKILLS

When you were younger, your parents and other adults decided what was best for your health. Now that you are older, you make many of these decisions for yourself. You take care of your personal health. You are developing your self-management skills. Two key self-management skills are practicing healthful behaviors and managing stress. When you eat healthy foods and get enough sleep, you are taking actions that promote good health. Stress management is learning to cope with challenges that put a strain on you mentally or emotionally.

Practicing Healthful Behaviors

Your behaviors affect your physical, mental/emotional, and social health. You will see benefits quickly when you practice healthful behaviors. If you exercise regularly, your heart and muscles grow stronger. When you eat healthful foods and drink plenty of water, your body works well.

Getting a good night's sleep will help you wake up with more energy. Respecting and caring for others will help you develop healthy relationships. Managing your feelings in positive ways will help you avoid actions you may regret later.

Staying **positive** is a **good health** *habit.*

Practicing healthful behaviors can help prevent injury, illness, and other health problems. When you practice healthful actions, you can help your total health. Your total health means your physical, mental/emotional, and social health. This means you take care of yourself and do not take risks. It means you learn health-promoting habits. When you eat well-balanced meals and

healthful snacks and get regular physical checkups you are practicing good health habits. Staying positive is another good health habit.

Managing Stress

Learning ways to deal with stress, *the body's response to real or imagined dangers or other life events,* is an important self-management skill. Stress management can help you learn ways to deal with stress. Stress management means identifying sources of stress. It also means you learn how to handle stress in ways that support good health. Relaxation is a good way to deal with stress. Exercise is another way to positively deal with stress.

Studying for a test can cause stress.

Making Decisions *and* Setting Goals

The path to good health begins with making good decisions. You may make more of your own decisions now. Some of those decisions might be deciding which clothes to buy or which classes to take.

As you grow older, you gain more freedom, but with it comes more responsibility. You will need to understand the short-term and long-term consequences of decisions.

Another responsibility is goal setting. You also need to plan how to reach those goals.

When you learn how to set realistic goals, you take a step toward health and well-being. Learning to make decisions and to set goals will help give you purpose and direction in your life.

ACCESSING INFORMATION

Knowing how to get **reliable,** or *trust-worthy and dependable,* health information is an important skill. Where can you find all this information? A main source is from adults you can trust. Community resources give you other ways to get information. These include the library and government health agencies. Organizations such as the American Red Cross can also provide good information.

Reliable Sources

You can find facts about health and health-enhancing products or services through media sources such as television, radio, and the Internet. TV and radio interviews with health professionals can give you information about current scientific studies related to health.

Web sites that end in .gov and .edu are often the most reliable sites. These sites are maintained by government organizations and educational institutions.

Getting health information is important, but so is analyzing whether that health information is valid, or reliable. Carefully review web sites ending in .org.

Many of these sites are maintained by organizations, such as the American Cancer Society or American Diabetes Association. However, some sites ending in .org may not be legitimate.

The Internet can be a good source of health information.

SW Productions/Getty Images

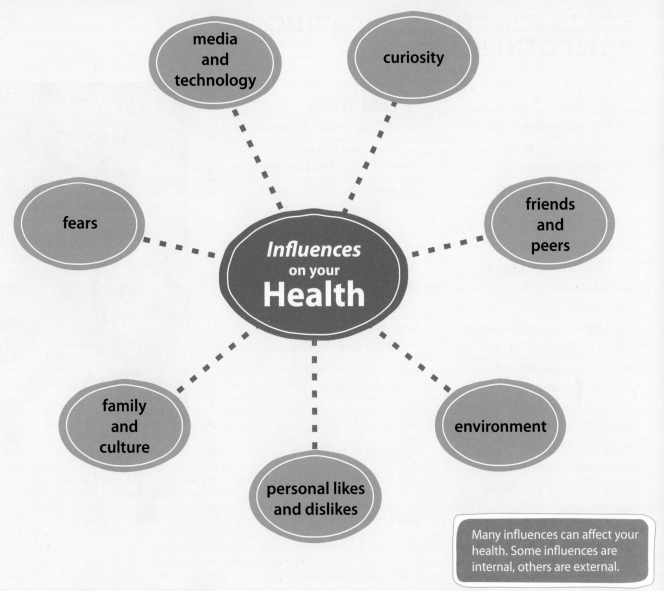

media and technology

curiosity

fears

Influences on your **Health**

friends and peers

family and culture

personal likes and dislikes

environment

Many influences can affect your health. Some influences are internal, others are external.

Analyzing Influences

Learning how to analyze health information, products, and services will help you act in ways that protect your health. The first step in analyzing an influence is to identify its source. A TV commercial may tell you a certain food has health benefits.

Your **decisions** have to do with your *own* **values** and **beliefs.**

Ask yourself who is the source of the information. Next, think about the motive, or reason, for the influence. Does the advertiser really take your well-being into consideration? Does the ad make you curious about the product?

Does it try to scare you into buying the product? Analyzing influences involves recognizing factors that affect or influence your health.

Your decisions also have to do with your own values and beliefs. The opinions of your friends and family members affect your decisions. Your culture and messages from the media also affect your decisions.

xix

SKILLS FOR COMMUNICATING WITH OTHERS

Your relationships with others depend on maintaining good communication skills. Communication is *the exchange of information through the use of words or actions.* Good communication skills include telling others how you feel. They also include listening to others and understanding how others feel. Two types of communication exist. They are verbal and nonverbal communication. Verbal communication involves a speaker or writer, and a listener or reader. Nonverbal communication includes tone of voice, body position, and using expressions.

Refusal Skills

An important communication skill is saying no. It may be something that is wrong. It may be something that you are not comfortable doing. You may worry what will happen if you don't go along with the group. Will your friends still like you? Will you still be a part of the group? It is at these times that refusal skills, or *strategies that help you say no effectively,* can help. Using refusal skills can sometimes be challenging, but they can help you stay true to yourself and to your beliefs. Also, other people will have respect for you for being honest.

Conflict Resolution

Conflicts, or disagreements with others, are part of life. Learning to deal with them in a healthy way is important. Conflict resolution is *a life skill that involves solving a disagreement in a way that satisfies both sides.* Conflict-resolution skills can help you find a way to satisfy everyone. Also, by using this positive health behavior, you can keep conflicts from getting out of hand.

Conflict **resolution** skills can help you find a way to *satisfy* **everyone.**

Advocacy

People with advocacy skills *take action in support of a cause.* They work to bring about a change by speaking out for something like health and wellness. When you speak out for health, you encourage other people to live healthy lives. Advocacy also means keeping others informed.

Using refusal skills effectively can help you avoid potentially dangerous situation.

Image Source/Getty Images

Making Decisions *and* Setting Goals

DECISIONS AND YOUR HEALTH

As you grow up, you usually gain more privileges. Along with privileges comes responsibility. You will make more of your own decisions. The choices and decisions you make can affect each part of your health triangle.

As you get older, you will learn to make more important decisions. You will need to understand the short-term and long-term consequences of the decisions you make.

You can learn the skill of making good decisions.

Some decisions may help you avoid harmful behaviors. These questions can help you understand some of the consequences of health-related decisions.

- How will this decision affect my health?
- Will it affect the health of others? If so, how?
- Is the behavior I might choose harmful or illegal?
- How will my family feel about my decision?
- Does this decision fit with my values?
- How will this decision affect my goals?

THE DECISION-MAKING PROCESS

You make decisions every day. Some decisions are easy to make. Other decisions are more difficult. Understanding the process of **decision making,** or *the process of making a choice or solving a problem,* will help you make the best possible decisions. The decision-making process can be broken down into six steps. You can apply these six steps to any decision you need to make.

Step 1: State the Situation

Identify the situation as you understand it. When you understand the situation and your choices you can make a sound decision. Ask yourself: What choice do you need to make? What are the facts? Who else is involved?

Step 2: List the Options

When you feel like you understand your situation, think of your options. List all of the possibilities you can think of. Be sure to include only those options that are safe. It is also important to ask an adult you trust for advice when making an important decision.

Step 3: Weigh the Possible Outcomes

After listing your options, you need to evaluate the consequences of each option. The word H.E.L.P. can be used to work through this step of the decision-making process.

- **H** (Healthful) What health risks will this option present to me and to others?
- **E** (Ethical) Does this choice reflect what my family and I believe to be ethical, or right? Does this choice show respect for me and others?
- **L** (Legal) Will I be breaking the law? Is this legal for someone my age?
- **P** (Parent Approval) Would my parents approve of this choice?

Step 4: Consider Your Values

Always consider your values or the beliefs that guide the way you live. Your values reflect what is important to you and what you have learned is right and wrong. Honesty, respect, consideration, and good health are values.

Step 5: Make a Decision and Act

You've weighed your options. You've considered the risks and consequences. Now you're ready for action. Choose the option that seems best for you. Remember that this step is not complete until you take action.

Step 6: Evaluate the Decision

Evaluating the results can help you make better decisions in the future. To evaluate the results, ask yourself: Was the outcome positive or negative? Were there any unexpected outcomes? Was there anything you could have done differently? How did your decision affect others? Do you think you made the right decision? What have you learned from the experience? If the outcome was not what you expected, try again.

Understanding the decision-making process will help you make sound decisions.

Step 1 State the situation.

Step 2 List the options.

Step 3 Weigh the possible outcomes.

Step 4 Consider your values.

Step 5 Make a decision and act.

Step 6 Evaluate the decision.

SETTING REALISTIC GOALS

When you think about your future, what do you see? Do you see someone who has graduated from college and has a good job? Are there things you want to achieve? Answering these questions can give you an idea of your goals in life. A goal is something you want to accomplish.

Goal setting is *the process of working toward something you want to accomplish.* When you have learned to set realistic goals, they can help you focus on what you want to accomplish in life. Realistic goals are goals you can reach.

Setting goals can benefit your health. Many goals can help to improve your overall health. Think about all you want to accomplish in life. Do you need to set some health-related goals to be able to accomplish those things?

Goals can become milestones and can tell you how far you have come. Reaching goals can be a powerful boost to your self-confidence. Improving your self-confidence can help to strengthen your mental/emotional health.

Types of Goals

There are two basic types of goals—short-term goals, *goals that you can achieve in a short length of time,* and long-term goals, *goals that you plan to reach over an extended period of time.* As the names imply, short-term goals can be accomplished more quickly than long-term goals.

Reaching *goals* can be a **powerful** *boost* to your **self confidence.**

Getting your homework turned in on time might be a short-term goal. Long-term goals are generally accomplished over months or years. Getting a college education might be a long-term goal. Often long-term goals are made up of short-term goals.

Reaching Your Goals

To accomplish your short-term and long-term goals, you need a plan. A goal-setting plan that has a series of steps for you to take can be very effective in helping you accomplish your goals. Following a plan can help you make the best use of your time, energy, and other resources. Here are the steps of a goal-setting plan:

- Step 1: Identify a specific goal and write it down. Write down exactly what your goal is. Be sure the goal is realistic.
- Step 2: List the steps to reach your goal. Breaking big goals into smaller goals can make them easier to accomplish.
- Step 3: Get help and support from others. There are many people in your life who can help you reach your goals. They may be parents, teachers, coaches, or other trusted adults.
- Step 4: Evaluate your progress. Check periodically to see if you are actually progressing toward your goal. You may have to identify and consider how to overcome an obstacle before moving toward your goal.
- Step 5: Celebrate when you reach your goal. Give yourself a reward.

Jamie has set a goal to be chosen for the all-star team

Choosing Health Services

WHAT IS HEALTH CARE?

You will probably at some point need to seek health care services. Health care provides services that promote, maintain, or restore health to individuals or communities. The health care system is all the medical care available to a nation's people, the way they receive the care, and the way the care is paid for. It is through the health care system that people receive medical services.

← Emergency

©Royalty-Free/Corbis

HEALTH CARE PROVIDERS

Many different professionals can help you with your health care. You may be most familiar with your own doctor who is your primary care provider: a health care professional who provides checkups and general care. Nurse practitioners and physician's assistants can also provide primary care.

In addition to doctors, nurse practitioners, and physician's assistants, many other health care professionals provide care. Nurses, pharmacists, health educators, counselors, mental health specialists, dentists, and nutritionists are all health care providers.

Preventive Care

Getting regular checkups is one way to prevent health problems and maintain wellness. During a checkup, your health care provider will check you carefully. She or he will check your heart and lungs and vision and hearing. You may also receive any immunizations you need. During your visit, your doctor may talk to you about healthful eating, exercise, avoiding alcohol, tobacco, and drugs, and other types of preventive care, or steps taken to keep disease or injury from happening or getting worse.

Specialists

Sometimes your primary care provider is not able to help you. In that case, he or she will refer you to a specialist, or health care professional trained to treat a special category of patients or specific health problems. Some specialists treat specific types of people. Other specialists treat specific conditions or body systems.

Different specialists treat different conditions.

Specialist	Specialty
Allergist	Asthma, hay fever, other allergies
Cardiologist	Heart problems
Dermatologist	Skin conditions and diseases
Oncologist	Cancer
Ophthalmologist	Eye diseases
Orthodontist	Tooth and jaw irregularities
Orthopedist	Broken bones and similar problems
Otolaryngologist	Ear, nose, and throat
Pediatrician	Infants, children, and teens

HEALTH CARE SETTINGS

Years ago, people were very limited as to where they could go for health care. In more recent years, new types of health care delivery settings have been developed. People now can go to their doctors' offices, hospitals, surgery centers, hospices, and assisted living communities.

Doctors' Offices

Doctors' offices are probably the most common setting for receiving health care. Your doctor, nurse practitioner, or physician's assistant has medical equipment to help them diagnose illnesses and to give checkups. Most of your medical needs can be met at your doctor's office.

Hospitals

If your medical needs cannot be met at your doctor's office, you may need to go to the hospital. Hospitals have much more medical equipment for diagnosing and treating illnesses. They have rooms for doing surgery and for emergency medicine. They have rooms for patients to stay overnight, if necessary. Hospitals have staff on duty around the clock every day of the year.

Surgery Centers

Your doctor may recommend that you go to a surgery center rather than a hospital. Surgery centers are facilities that offer outpatient surgical care. This means that the patients do not stay overnight. They go home the same day they have the surgery. Serious surgeries cannot be done in a surgery center. They would be done in a hospital where the patient can stay and recover. For general outpatient care, many people go to clinics.

Clinics

Clinics are similar to doctors' offices and often have primary care physicians and specialists on staff. If you go to a clinic, you might not see the same doctor each time you go. You might see whoever is on duty that day. This might make it more difficult for the doctor to get to know you and your health issues. However, for people who do not need to go to the doctor often, a clinic might be a good fit.

Hospice Care

Hospice care provides a place where terminally ill patients can live out the remainder of their lives. Terminally ill patients will not recover from their illness. Hospice workers are specially trained and are experts in pain management. They are also trained and skilled at giving emotional support to the family and the patient. Many terminally ill patients receive hospice care in their own homes. Nurses visit the patient in their own home and provide medications for pain. They also spend time with family members, helping them learn to cope during the emotionally difficult time.

Assisted Living Communities

As people get older, they may not be able to take care of themselves as well as they used to. Assisted living communities offer older people an alternative to nursing homes. In nursing homes, all of the resident's needs are taken care of. In assisted living communities, the residents can choose which services they need. They may be unable to drive and need transportation. They may need reminders to take medications. They may need to have food prepared for them. In an assisted living community, the residents are able to live in their own apartments as long as they are able. Medical staff is available when the residents need help.

PAYING FOR HEALTH CARE

Health care costs can be expensive. Many people buy health insurance to help pay for medical costs. Health insurance is a plan in which a person pays a set fee to an insurance company in return for the company's agreement to pay some or all medical expenses when needed. They pay a monthly premium, or fee, to the health insurance company for the policy. There are several different options when choosing health insurance.

Private Health Care Plans

One health insurance option is managed care. Health insurance plans emphasize preventative medicine and work to control the cost and maintain the quality of health care. Using managed care, patients save money when they visit doctors who participate in the managed care plan. There are several different managed care plans such as a health maintenance organization (HMO), a preferred provider organization (PPO), and a point-of-service (POS) plan.

Government Public Health Care Plans

The government currently offers two types of health insurance—Medicaid and Medicare. Medicaid is for people with limited income. Medicare is for people over the age of 65 and for people of any age with certain disabilities.

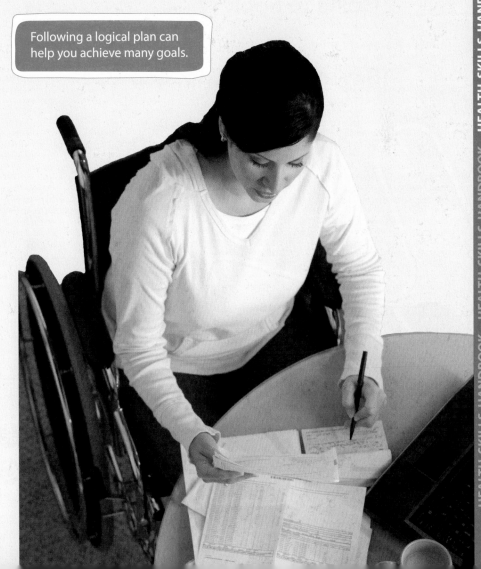

Following a logical plan can help you achieve many goals.

Tobacco

LESSONS

 **PREMIUM ONLINE RESOURCES** ⟩

 Audio

 Videos

 Bilingual Glossary

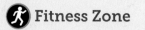 Fitness Zone

Web Quest

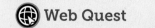 Review

Tobacco use can pose serious risks to your health. *What are some of the consequences of using tobacco?*

Facts About Tobacco

BIG IDEA The substances contained in tobacco products are very harmful to your health.

Before You Read

QUICK WRITE Make a list of as many tobacco products as you can think of prior to reading this lesson. Briefly describe each product.

▶ Video

As You Read

FOLDABLES Study Organizer

Make the Foldable® on page 86 to record the information presented in Lesson 1.

Vocabulary

> nicotine
> addictive
> smokeless tobacco
> snuff
> tar
> bronchi
> carbon monoxide

🔊 Audio

🔤 Bilingual Glossary

Myth vs. Fact

Myth: Cigarettes advertised as "all natural" are safer to smoke than regular cigarettes.

Fact: All cigarettes are harmful to the human body. The smoke from any cigarette contains tar and carbon monoxide. There is no evidence that any type of cigarette is less harmful than another.

WHAT IS TOBACCO?

MAIN IDEA Tobacco is a harmful and addictive substance in all its forms.

Tobacco is a woody, shrub-like plant with large leaves. It is grown throughout the world. Tobacco contains harmful substances that are released when a person smokes or chews it. Tobacco companies add more harmful ingredients when they prepare tobacco to be sold. It is estimated that there are more than 4,000 chemicals in tobacco—many of which have been proven to cause cancer. Some of the same ingredients found in cleaning products or pest poisons are added to tobacco products.

Forms of Tobacco

Tobacco companies harvest leaves from tobacco plants. The leaves are then prepared for smoking or chewing. Tobacco products come in many forms. The most common include cigarettes, cigars, pipes, specialty cigarettes, and smokeless tobacco.

CIGARETTES These are the most commonly used forms of tobacco products. Cigarettes contain shredded tobacco leaves. They may also have filters intended to block some harmful chemicals. However, filters do not remove enough chemicals to make cigarettes less dangerous. Also, some tobacco users may try not to inhale the smoke, but smoking in any form is not safe for your body.

There are more than *4,000* **chemicals in tobacco.**

Tobacco smoke contains many harmful chemicals that put smokers at risk for lung diseases, heart disease, and various types of cancer. Tobacco also contains nicotine, *an addictive, or habit forming, drug.* **Addictive** means *capable of causing a user to develop intense cravings.* These cravings make it hard to quit.

Nicotine is found in all types of cigarettes, cigars, pipe tobacco, and smokeless tobacco. The nicotine in tobacco products is so addictive that most users find it very difficult to stop using tobacco once they start. You will learn more about nicotine addiction and ways to avoid tobacco later in this chapter.

CIGARS AND PIPES As is the case with cigarettes, the tobacco used in cigars and pipes is made up of shredded tobacco leaves. However, one large cigar can contain as much tobacco and nicotine as an entire pack of 20 cigarettes. Pipes and cigars also cause some of the same serious health problems that cigarettes do. Cigar smoke contains up to 90 times more cancer-causing chemicals than those found in cigarette smoke. People who smoke cigars or pipes are more likely to develop mouth, tongue, or lip cancer than people who do not use tobacco. Cigar and pipe smokers also face an increased risk of dying from heart disease compared to nonsmokers.

SPECIALTY CIGARETTES

This category includes flavored, unfiltered cigarettes and clove cigarettes. Flavored cigarettes are typically imported from other countries. In addition to clove, some have added flavors such as cherry, strawberry, or cinnamon. The U.S. has tried to ban sales of flavored cigarettes in an effort to discourage young people from trying them. Flavored tobacco is also smoked in special water pipes called hookahs. These forms of tobacco contain higher concentrations of harmful chemicals than do regular cigarettes.

ELECTRONIC CIGARETTES

These products look like regular cigarettes. "E-cigarettes" do not contain tobacco, but they still have nicotine inside. Liquid nicotine is heated, and users inhale the vapor. These "smokeless cigarettes" are sometimes marketed as a way to help smokers quit or as an alternative to regular cigarettes. However, the nicotine in electronic cigarettes has the same harmful addictive effects as that found in regular cigarettes.

SMOKELESS TOBACCO

Smokeless tobacco is *ground tobacco that is chewed, placed inside the mouth along the gum line, or inhaled through the nose.* It comes in two forms. Chewing tobacco is often called "dip" or "spit tobacco." Snuff is *finely ground tobacco that is inhaled or held in the mouth or cheeks.* While it does not affect the lungs the way smoking does, smokeless tobacco is not a safe alternative to cigarettes. It contains addictive nicotine and other chemicals and causes gum disease and oral cancer.

>>> **Reading Check**

IDENTIFY *What are the most common health risks associated with cigars and pipes?*

Sports leagues have restricted the use of smokeless tobacco by athletes. *Describe the influence this might have on sports fans.*

CHEMICALS IN TOBACCO

MAIN IDEA Tobacco contains many chemicals that can harm your body.

Harmful chemical compounds exist in all forms of tobacco. These are released when a person smokes or chews tobacco. Chemicals in tobacco can also affect nonsmokers who inhale others' smoke. Most of these chemicals hurt your body's ability to work properly.

Harmful chemicals exist in all forms of *tobacco.*

- **Nicotine** is one of the harmful substances found in tobacco leaves and in all tobacco products. Nicotine is an addictive, or habit-forming, drug. A person begins to depend on it after it has been in the body regularly. A person can become addicted to nicotine very quickly. Nicotine has other effects, too. It makes your heart beat faster and raises your blood pressure. It causes dizziness and an upset stomach and reduces the amount of oxygen your blood carries to the brain.

- **Tar** is *a dark, thick liquid that forms when tobacco burns.* When a person smokes, the smoker inhales this dangerous substance. When it is inhaled, tar covers the airways and the **bronchi,** which *are passageways that branch from the trachea to each lung.* Lungs covered with tar can become diseased and cause serious breathing trouble.

- **Carbon monoxide** is *a colorless, odorless, poisonous gas that is created when tobacco burns.* Carbon monoxide harms the brain and the heart by reducing the amount of oxygen available to these organs. If too much carbon monoxide enters your body, it can kill you.

>>> **Reading Check**

NAME *What are three harmful substances found in tobacco smoke?* ■

Smoking tobacco in cigarettes is one way people are at risk of getting cancer or having other health problems. *Explain some of the healthful decision can you make about tobacco.*

REVIEW

>>>**After You Read**

1. **VOCABULARY** What does the term *addictive* mean? Use it in a complete sentence.
2. **SUMMARIZE** Why is tobacco harmful?
3. **IDENTIFY** Name three substances in tobacco smoke that are harmful to the body.

>>> **Thinking Critically**

4. **ANALYZE** If many cigarettes have filters, why are they still not safe?
5. **EXPLAIN** What is harmful about the chemicals in tobacco?

>>> **Applying Health Skills**

6. **COMMUNICATION SKILLS** Ryan has learned that his friend Spencer smokes cigars and uses smokeless tobacco. Spencer tells Ryan that this is not as bad as smoking cigarettes. What facts might you suggest that Ryan share with Spencer to convince him that his tobacco use is still harmful?

🔄 Review
🔊 Audio

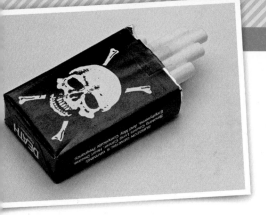

Health Risks *of* Tobacco Use

BIG IDEA Tobacco is a dangerous drug with serious health consequences.

Before You Read

QUICK WRITE List two future goals. Then write a short paragraph telling how a tobacco-related illness could affect each of these goals.

▶ Video

As You Read

STUDY ORGANIZER Make the study organizer on page 86 to record the information presented in Lesson 2.

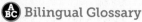

Vocabulary

› alveoli
› emphysema

🔊 Audio

🔤 Bilingual Glossary

What Teens Want to Know

Will smoking make my skin look worse? Smoking cigarettes causes changes in the skin that speed up the aging process. Only sun exposure does more damage to the skin than smoking. A research study found microscopic wrinkles developing on the skin of smokers as young as 20 years old. In addition, a smoker's skin tends to develop a yellowish or grayish look.

TOBACCO USE IS HARMFUL TO YOUR HEALTH

MAIN IDEA Health experts have been warning about the dangers of tobacco for many years.

The message that smoking is bad for your health is not new. In 1964, the Surgeon General issued a report saying that smoking may be hazardous. A year later, tobacco companies were ordered to add health warnings to cigarette packages. Since then, the warning labels have become more prominent. Other tobacco products now also carry similar warnings.

Tobacco use has serious consequences. The chemicals in tobacco and tobacco smoke can cause damage to most of the body's systems. In the United States, more than 400,000 people die every year from smoking-related illnesses. Tobacco use is especially damaging to teens because their bodies are still growing. The chemicals in tobacco interfere with this process of growth and development.

You have already learned that nicotine raises the heart rate and blood pressure. Tobacco users often cannot run as long or as fast as they did before they started smoking. They get sick more often and tend to stay sick longer. Tobacco use can cause diseases of the mouth and lungs.

400,000 people *die* every year from **smoking-related illnesses.**

Tobacco use also damages the rest of the body. It can cause diseases of the circulatory system, respiratory system, nervous system, digestive system, and excretory system. Many of these illnesses can be prevented if you choose the positive health behavior of staying tobacco free.

›››› Reading Check

RECALL *Why is smoking especially hazardous to teen health?*

Respiratory System	Tobacco smoke damages the air sacs in the lungs. This damage can lead to a life-threatening disease that destroys these air sacs. Smokers are also between 12 and 22 times more likely than nonsmokers to develop lung cancer.
Digestive System	All forms of tobacco increase the risk of cavities and gum disease. Tobacco dulls the taste buds and can cause stomach ulcers. Tobacco use is linked to cancers of the mouth, throat, stomach, esophagus, and pancreas.
Nervous System	Tobacco use reduces the flow of oxygen to the brain, which can lead to a stroke.
Excretory System	Smokers have at least twice the risk of developing bladder cancer as nonsmokers. Smokeless tobacco can also put users at risk of developing bladder cancer.
Circulatory System	Tobacco use is linked to heart disease. It increases the chances of a heart attack. Smoking also raises blood pressure and heart rate.

Respiratory System

Tobacco smoke contains tar, which coats the inside of the lungs. Smoke damages the alveoli, or *tiny air sacs in the lungs.* When this happens, your lungs are less able to supply oxygen to your body. This damage can cause emphysema, *a disease that results in the destruction of the alveoli in the lungs.* When this disease affects a large part of the lungs, it can cause death.

The chemicals in tobacco also put smokers at a greatly increased risk of developing lung cancer. Lung cancer is the leading cause of death among people who smoke. A person who quits smoking completely can greatly reduce the risk of lung cancer.

A person who **quits smoking** can *reduce the risk* of **lung cancer.**

Circulatory System

Tobacco use affects the circulatory or cardiovascular system, which includes the heart and blood vessels. As nicotine enters the circulatory system, blood vessels constrict, or squeeze together. Over time, the blood vessels can harden. When this happens, the blood vessels cannot carry enough oxygen and nutrients to all the parts of the body that need them.

Using tobacco harms many body systems, causing many health problems or diseases. *Explain the effects of tobacco use on the digestive system.*

Tobacco use also raises blood pressure and heart rate. Blood vessels narrow and harden due to nicotine and other factors. As a result, the heart has to work harder to move blood, oxygen, and nutrients through the body. When the heart has to work harder and blood vessels are narrower, blood pressure goes up. High blood pressure puts more stress on the heart and blood vessels. This increases the chance of a heart attack, stroke, or heart disease.

Nervous System

Your brain needs oxygen. The carbon monoxide in tobacco smoke can cut down the amount of oxygen that the blood can carry to the brain. Nicotine reaches the brain in only a few seconds and attaches to special receptors in brain cells. The brain then adapts by increasing the number of nicotine receptors. Tobacco users then have a strong need for more tobacco.

Digestive System

Smoking can damage your digestive system. It can lead to mouth and stomach ulcers, which are painful, open sores. People with ulcers may not be able to eat certain foods. They may not get all the nutrition they need. Smoking also harms teeth and gums, causing teeth to yellow. Smokers are also more likely to get cavities and gum disease.

Excretory System

Tobacco can also harm your excretory system. Smokers and tobacco users are much more likely to develop bladder cancer than are nonsmokers. Chemicals in tobacco smoke are absorbed from the lungs and get into the blood. From the blood, the chemicals get into the kidneys and bladder. These chemicals damage the kidneys and the cells that line the inside of the bladder and increase the risk of cancer. Smoking tobacco is also a factor in the development of colorectal cancer, a cancer that affects the colon and the rectum.

>>> **Reading Check**

SUMMARIZE *List two harmful effects of smoking tobacco.*

The first photo is a healthy lung. The second photo is a cancerous lung. Healthy lungs provide oxygen to your body. *Evaluate the choices you can make to decrease your risk of getting lung cancer.*

Health SKILLS ACTIVITY

Decision Making

Fresh-Air *Friend*

Mike gets a ride to school with his friend Ashley and her mom. Mike is concerned because Ashley's mom smokes in the car. He hasn't mentioned it because he doesn't want to sound ungrateful. He has tried opening a window, but Ashley says it makes her cold. Mike doesn't know what to do or say. Use the decision-making process to help Mike make a decision.

* State the situation.

* Consider your values.

* List the options.

* Make a decision and act.

* Weight the possible outcomes.

* Evaluate the decision.

Apply the six steps of the decision-making process to Mike's problem. What are Mike's options? Show how Mike makes a healthful decision.

EFFECTS OF TOBACCO USE

MAIN IDEA Tobacco use causes both short-term and long-term damage to the body.

Tobacco use causes changes in the body. Some of the effects of tobacco use are immediate. These short-term effects can often be felt right away.

- **Cravings** Nicotine is a very addictive drug, which means it causes the body to want more of it. A person who uses tobacco may feel a need for more very soon after using it.
- **Breathing and heart rate** For a smoker, it becomes harder to breathe during normal physical activity. It is more difficult for a tobacco user to work out for a long period of time. Nicotine also causes the heart to beat faster than normal.

Tobacco use causes **changes** in **the body.**

- **Taste and appetite** Tobacco use dulls taste buds and reduces appetite. Tobacco users may lose much of their ability to enjoy food. However, when a person quits using tobacco, taste buds will heal.
- **Unpleasant feelings** Tobacco users may experience dizziness. Their hands and feet may also feel colder than normal.
- **Unattractive effects** Tobacco use causes bad breath, yellowed teeth, and smelly hair, skin, and clothes. It also ages the skin more quickly.

As you have learned, the chemicals in tobacco cause damage to many body systems. The impact of tobacco use is not limited only to smokers and other tobacco users. Simply being around other people who smoke can also cause health problems. Some of the long-term damage caused by tobacco use can even be life-threatening.

- **Bronchitis** Tobacco smoke can damage the bronchi, or the passages through which air travels to the lungs. Also, a buildup of tar in the lungs can cause a smoker to have fits of uncontrollable coughing.
- **Emphysema** This disease can make a person use most of his or her energy just to breathe. Emphysema is a common cause of death for smokers.
- **Lung cancer** Nearly 90 percent of lung cancer deaths are caused by smoking.
- **Heart disease** The nicotine in tobacco greatly increases the risk of heart attack or stroke.
- **Weakened immune system** Long-term tobacco use harms the body's defenses against various diseases. Tobacco users are also more likely to get common illnesses such as coughs, colds, and allergies.

>>> **Reading Check**

DESCRIBE *What are two long-term and short-term effects of tobacco use?* ■

REVIEW

>>> **After You Read**

1. **DEFINE** What does *emphysema* mean? Use it in an original sentence.
2. **SUMMARIZE** Describe the ways in which smoking harms the systems in the body.
3. **IDENTIFY** What is the leading cause of death among people who smoke?

>>> **Thinking Critically**

4. **ANALYZE** Which of the health risks associated with tobacco use do you consider the most serious? Explain your answer.
5. **APPLY** Bethany is at a party where another girl lights a cigarette. When Bethany points out that smoking is bad for her health, the other girl shrugs. "I'm a strong person," she says. "I can quit any time I want to." How might Bethany reply?

>>> **Applying Health Skills**

6. **ACCESS INFORMATION** Conduct more research into the harmful effects of tobacco. Use health journals, magazines, and web sites of national organizations. Write a short report about the information you find.

Ⓖ Review

🔊 Audio

Tobacco Addiction

BIG IDEA Tobacco contains nicotine, which is an extremely powerful and addictive drug.

Before You Read

QUICK WRITE Make a list of habits you know are hard to break. Choose one that interests you and write a paragraph describing what you think it would be like to change that habit.

 Video

As You Read

STUDY ORGANIZER Make the study organizer on page 86 to record the information presented in Lesson 3.

Vocabulary

› addiction
› psychological dependence
› physical dependence
› tolerance
› withdrawal
› relapse

 Audio

ABC Bilingual Glossary

Cultural Literacy

Smokeless Tobacco Smokeless tobacco includes chewing tobacco and a finely ground tobacco known as snuff. The CDC has found that about 11 percent of teen boys and 2.2 percent of teen girls have used smokeless tobacco. However, it is not a safer alternative to smoking. Smokeless tobacco causes a variety of health problems, including white patches in the mouth that can lead to oral cancer.

A POWERFUL DRUG

MAIN IDEA Tobacco contains strong substances that make it difficult to stop using once a person has started.

Many people know the dangers of tobacco use, but they continue to use it over many years. As you have learned, tobacco contains nicotine. Nicotine is a powerful drug that causes addiction, or *a mental or physical need for a drug or other substance.* Scientific studies have shown that nicotine is as addictive as powerful drugs such as cocaine or heroin. This addiction is both psychological and physical.

The Path *to* Addiction

When nicotine enters the body, it interacts with receptors in the tobacco user's brain. The brain sends a message to the body to speed up heart and breathing rates. As heart and breathing rates return to normal, the user wanting more. Tobacco use soon becomes a habit, and a user can quickly become addicted.

Nicotine is as **addictive** as powerful drugs such as **cocaine** or **heroin.**

Studies have shown that as many as 90 percent of adult smokers began using tobacco before the age of 18. Teens are more likely to develop a severe level of addiction than people who begin smoking at a later age. Teens who use tobacco are also much more likely to use drugs such as marijuana, cocaine, and alcohol. For example, a recent national survey shows that more than 90 percent of cocaine users smoked cigarettes before they started using cocaine. Another study has shown that nicotine addiction may lead to other addictions.

Reading Check

DESCRIBE *Why is it especially risky for teens to try tobacco?*

Tobacco use leads to nicotine addiction. Once a person is addicted to the nicotine in tobacco, it becomes very difficult to quit. Here are some facts about how people become addicted to tobacco use:

- The government has found that tobacco companies market to young people. Some people start using tobacco as early as age 11 or 12.
- Research has shown that every day in the United States, more than 6,000 teens and preteens try their first cigarette or other form of tobacco.

- Teens can feel symptoms of nicotine addiction only days or weeks after they first start using tobacco. The symptoms of addiction are felt even before teens start to use tobacco regularly. This can be especially harmful since the teen years are a time of rapid growth and development.
- The earlier in life someone tries tobacco, the higher the chances that person will become a regular tobacco user. Early tobacco use also lowers the chances a person will ever be able to quit.

The best way to prevent tobacco addiction is to never start using tobacco. *Explain why it is difficult to stop smoking once a person has started.*

Health SKILLS ACTIVITY

Accessing Information

Quitting *Tobacco Use*

A person's physical dependence on nicotine makes it very hard to quit using tobacco. Some people cannot quit on their own. Sometimes they need help to overcome the physical addiction to nicotine. Two common methods for quitting are nicotine replacement and certain medications.

* Nicotine replacement may involve nicotine gum, patches, or lozenges for tobacco users over age 18. Adults don't need a prescription for these treatments. You do need a prescription for nicotine inhalers and nasal sprays.

* People who want to quit smoking may join support groups. They can find suggestions about how to stop from organizations such as the American Heart Association or the American Lung Association.

On Your Own

Use various resources to find valid information about a method of quitting tobacco use. Create an informative brochure covering how the method works and how it helps people deal with cravings for nicotine. Present your brochure to the class.

Janis Christie/Getty Images

Physical *and* Psychological Dependence

Psychological dependence is *a person's belief that he or she needs a drug to feel good or act normally.* In other words, the desire for tobacco becomes greater than the fear of its dangers. **Physical dependence** is *an addiction in which the body develops a chemical need for a drug.* This can happen quickly for a person who uses tobacco. Teens can develop a physical dependence for nicotine even more easily than adults.

The *desire* for tobacco **becomes greater** than the *fear* of its dangers.

As you have learned, nicotine is a drug. As with any drug, the body will develop a **tolerance,** or *a need for larger and larger amounts of a drug to produce the same effect.* This grows over time and causes a tobacco user to crave nicotine. Anyone who quits tobacco goes through **withdrawal.** This is *a series of symptoms a person experiences when he or she stops using an addictive substance.* When a person goes through withdrawal from tobacco, cravings for nicotine typically increase. Someone who is trying to quit may also have mood changes, feel nervous or irritable, or be extra hungry.

The body undergoes physical changes when a person no longer uses tobacco. For example, the nicotine and carbon monoxide from tobacco are replaced by more oxygen in the blood. The extra oxygen is healthier for the body, but it may affect the brain and result in headaches or dizziness for a while. The extra oxygen in the blood may also cause a person who has quit to feel tingling in the fingers or toes. Since nicotine acts as a stimulant, someone who has stopped using tobacco may suddenly feel extra tired or sleepy.

Sometimes, the symptoms of nicotine withdrawal are so bad that a person starts using tobacco again. Many people who stop smoking have a **relapse,** which is *a return to the use of a drug.* Relapses are common during the first few months after a tobacco user quits.

The physical and psychological effects of withdrawal may lead a person to return to nicotine. However, if someone starts smoking again after working hard to quit tobacco, it can leave that person frustrated and angry. As a result, many people try to quit several times before they finally break the habit. Fortunately, many resources are available to help people either say no to tobacco before they start or to help them kick the habit for good.

>>> **Reading Check**

DESCRIBE *What are the symptoms of nicotine withdrawal?* ■

>>> **After You Read**

1. **DEFINE** What does the term *addiction* mean? Use it in a complete sentence.
2. **IDENTIFY** What is the substance in tobacco that causes addiction?
3. **RECALL** Explain the difference between physical dependence and psychological dependence.

>>> **Thinking Critically**

4. **SYNTHESIZE** Explain how a person becomes addicted to tobacco.
5. **ANALYZE** Why do you think it is important for a teen never to try tobacco?

>>> **Applying Health Skills**

6. **REFUSAL SKILLS** Some teens try tobacco for the first time because of peer pressure. With a small group, brainstorm effective ways to say no when peers offer or suggest that you use tobacco. Make a list of the best ideas and share them with your class.

Ⓒ Review

🔊 Audio

Costs *to* Society

BIG IDEA Tobacco has consequences in addition to the harm it causes tobacco users.

Before You Read

QUICK WRITE Make a list of the costs associated with tobacco use. As you read, add costs to your list.

▶ Video

As You Read

STUDY ORGANIZER Make the study organizer found in the FL pages in the back of the book to record the information presented in Lesson 4.

Vocabulary

› secondhand smoke
› mainstream smoke
› sidestream smoke
› passive smoker

🔊 Audio

🔤 Bilingual Glossary

Developing Good Character

Citizenship Good citizens look out for the welfare of the community. The term *community* includes more than just your neighborhood. It also includes the environment and the air you breathe. Obeying laws that regulate smoking is one way of showing good citizenship. Brainstorm ways of showing good citizenship when it comes to tobacco.

TOBACCO'S MANY COSTS

MAIN IDEA Tobacco use is costly to society.

You have learned about how harmful it is to use tobacco. Unfortunately, tobacco use includes many more costs. Society as a whole pays a price, and people who do not use tobacco may also experience health problems as a result. For example, tobacco companies spend more than $34 million each day on marketing to encourage people to use tobacco products. Whether or not they use tobacco, U.S. taxpayers pay billions of dollars each year in federal taxes to treat the many health problems caused by tobacco use. In addition, many more costs and consequences are associated with tobacco use.

Costs *to* Smokers

Tobacco use is expensive. Researchers have determined that the average cigarette smoker uses one-and-a-half packs each day. The average price per pack in most states has risen to more than $5.

This means the typical smoker spends more than $8 per day on cigarettes. That adds up to $250 over the course of one month, or $3,000 per year. In ten years' time, the average smoker in the U.S. will have spent more than $30,000 on cigarettes.

Society as a whole *pays a price* as a result of **tobacco use.**

Tobacco users also spend more money on health care. They pay higher health insurance rates than nonsmokers. Tobacco users can also expect to live shorter lives and have more health problems than people who do not use tobacco. This is especially true for females. Tobacco use shortens a woman's life by an average of five years. Fires are another health risk posed by smoking. Tobacco left burning is often the cause of fires at home. Carelessly discarded cigarettes or matches can also spark wildfires.

Getty Images/Tetra images RF/fotog

Costs to Nonsmokers

Even if you do not smoke, being around those who do can be harmful. Whenever people smoke near you, you breathe *air that has been contaminated by tobacco smoke* called secondhand smoke or environmental tobacco smoke (ETS). Secondhand smoke is filled with nicotine, carbon monoxide, and other harmful substances.

Secondhand smoke comes in two forms: mainstream smoke and sidestream smoke. Mainstream smoke is the *smoke that is inhaled and then exhaled by a smoker.* Sidestream smoke is *smoke that comes from the burning end of a cigarette, pipe, or cigar.* The U.S. Environmental Protection Agency (EPA) has labeled secondhand smoke as a human carcinogen. This means it causes cancer.

Even if you **do not smoke,** being around those who do can be harmful.

A passive smoker is *a nonsmoker who breathes in secondhand smoke.* Adults who do not use tobacco but who regularly breathe secondhand smoke can get sick from it. They can have the same health problems as smokers. An estimated 46,000 nonsmokers die each year from heart disease. About 3,000 additional nonsmokers die of lung cancer each year.

Secondhand smoke is especially harmful to young children and people with asthma. When children are exposed to secondhand smoke, they are more likely to have respiratory and other health problems. Allergies, asthma, ear infections, bronchitis, pneumonia, and heart problems have all been linked to exposure to secondhand smoke.

Secondhand smoke is dangerous to everyone's health. *Evaluate why smoke-free restaurants are considered to be healthier for customers and restaurant workers.*

Costs to Unborn Children

Women who use tobacco while pregnant put their unborn children in serious danger. Their babies could be born too early or too small or even die. The lower a baby's birth weight, the higher the chances that the baby will have health problems. Sudden infant death syndrome (SIDS) is linked to babies whose mothers smoked during or after pregnancy. Babies who are born to mothers who used tobacco while pregnant may also grow and develop more slowly than other children. This can cause health issues throughout childhood.

Costs to Society

Tobacco not only harms the body, it costs the user and society a lot of money. Smoking and other forms of tobacco use have hidden costs. Two additional costs involved in tobacco use are:

- **Lost productivity.** Productivity is how much a person is able to finish in the time he or she works. People who use tobacco have lower productivity levels on the job. They are sick more often than nonsmokers and get less done. Lost productivity costs businesses a lot of money. The nation as a whole pays a large price too. The government estimates that smoking costs the U.S. economy $96 billion per year in lost productivity.

- **Health care costs.** People who use tobacco tend to need more medical treatment than those who do not. If tobacco users have health insurance, it may help pay for some of their treatment. However, because health insurance companies face more costs to cover tobacco users, they charge higher rates for their insurance. If a tobacco user has no health insurance, the government helps cover the costs. This means that every family in the U.S. pays for tobacco use through their taxes.

>>> **Reading Check**

IDENTIFY *Name three groups of people affected by tobacco use.*

Thank You For Not Smoking

C Squared Studios/Getty Images

COUNTERING THE COSTS OF TOBACCO USE

MAIN IDEA Laws and education protect nonsmokers and lower the cost of tobacco use to society.

According to the U.S. Centers for Disease Control and Prevention, each pack of cigarettes sold results in more than $10 in added costs for health care and lost productivity. Some public action groups and Congress have investigated ways to lower these costs. New laws have been proposed that would restrict or even ban the manufacture and sale of tobacco products. Many smokers, however, claim that such restrictions would interfere with their constitutional rights.

Tobacco Taxes

One important action has been taken to reduce the cost of tobacco use to society. Taxes are now added to each pack of cigarettes sold in the United States and in certain states. For example, there is a federal excise tax that adds $1 to the price of each pack of cigarettes.

Additional taxes make it more costly to buy tobacco products and give the government more money to educate people about the dangers of tobacco use.

> **Each pack of cigarettes** sold results in more than *$10* in **added costs** for **health care** and **lost productivity.**

Smoke-Free Environments

Many state and local governments have tried to lower the cost to nonsmokers through laws that ban smoking in public spaces. This protects nonsmokers from dangerous secondhand smoke. It has become common to find businesses and restaurants where smoking indoors or even outdoors is not allowed. These laws protect the health of all restaurant patrons.

Some towns and cities have even made it illegal to smoke in certain outdoor locations, such as beaches, playgrounds, and gardens. The federal government has also passed laws to protect the rights of nonsmokers. For example, since 1989, it has been illegal to smoke on all airplane flights in the United States.

Labeling Laws *and* Advertising Limits

Laws now control the ways that tobacco companies are allowed to market and sell tobacco products. Cigarette packages must have clear warning labels, or disclaimers. The disclaimers state clearly that smoking is harmful. Cans and pouches of smokeless tobacco must also display similar disclaimers. The same laws apply to advertisements for tobacco.

Limits on tobacco advertising are more extensive than ever before. In the United States, laws protect young people from tobacco advertisements. For example, tobacco companies cannot place outdoor ads within 1,000 feet of schools and playgrounds or advertise on television or radio. They cannot make or sell promotional hats, T-shirts, and other items. This is why tobacco companies try to place their products in the media being used by celebrities. It allows them to work around the laws in place.

SURGEON GENERAL'S WARNING: Smoking Causes Lung Cancer, Heart Disease, Emphysema, And May Complicate Pregnancy.

Federal law requires that cigarette packages have one of four different warning labels. *Describe the goal of tobacco warning labels.*

Debora Cartagena/CDC

Antismoking Campaigns

Anti-tobacco ads are helping create awareness about the dangers of tobacco use. The goal is to send a message to people of every age that using tobacco is a risk behavior. Antismoking ads also explain that tobacco use has many negative consequences. Smokers who see these ads may recognize the dangers of tobacco. As a result, they may quit or seek treatment. The ads can help non-smokers recognize the benefits of remaining tobacco free.

Antismoking ads are helping **create awareness** about the **dangers of tobacco use.**

State and local governments are also making efforts to stop tobacco use. Most communities enforce laws against selling tobacco to minors. Smoking is often prohibited on school grounds. States have sued tobacco companies to recover costs to the public related to tobacco use. Part of the money awarded in these cases has helped fund anti-tobacco campaigns. Many communities plan activities to promote healthy lifestyles. Individuals can also help to stop or limit tobacco use. You can do your part by encouraging others to avoid tobacco use.

>>> **Reading Check**

SUMMARIZE *What actions have been taken to lower the cost to society of tobacco use?* ■

Smoke free areas in the community help promote healthy lifestyles. *Describe how no smoking signs placed throughout the community can help promote healthy lifestyles.*

REVIEW

>>> **After You Read**

1. **DEFINE** Explain what the terms *sidestream smoke* and *mainstream smoke* mean. Use both terms in complete sentences.
2. **IDENTIFY** What health care costs are involved with tobacco use?
3. **DESCRIBE** Explain the effects smoking can have on unborn babies and children.

>>> **Thinking Critically**

4. **ANALYZE** How can laws to protect you from secondhand smoke help to protect your health?
5. **EXPLAIN** What solutions have been offered for the problems of tobacco use? Explain how these solutions seem to help lower the costs of tobacco use to society.

>>> **Applying Health Skills**

6. **ACCESS INFORMATION** Research the latest government restrictions on tobacco companies or advertisements. Write a paragraph describing your findings.

↻ Review

🔊 Audio

Saying No *to* Tobacco Use

BIG IDEA It is important to have strategies to resist the strong influences around tobacco use.

Before You Read

QUICK WRITE Write a short dialogue between yourself and a peer who wants you to try tobacco. Show how you can politely but firmly refuse.

 Video

As You Read

STUDY ORGANIZER Make the study organizer on page 86 to record the information presented in Lesson 5.

Vocabulary

› target audience
› product placement
› point-of-sale promotion
› cold turkey
› nicotine replacement therapies

 Audio

🔤 Bilingual Glossary

🏃 Fitness Zone

Fitness Calendar To stay healthy and tobacco free, it helps me to have an activity calendar. I can set goals for how much physical activity I want to get each day. When I choose new activities to try, it makes it more interesting. I also like to use an online diary to keep track of how well I am doing with my goal.

WHY DO TEENS USE TOBACCO?

MAIN IDEA Many sources can influence teens to try tobacco.

With all the risks you have read about in this chapter, you may wonder why any teen would use tobacco. Many influences pressure teens to try tobacco or make it look appealing. In this lesson, you will learn more about those factors and about ways to stay tobacco free.

Influence *of* Peers *and* Family

Peer pressure is one of the major reasons that teens try tobacco. People are more likely to use tobacco if their friends use it. Some teens use tobacco in order to fit in with their friends. Others use tobacco because they think it makes them seem cooler or more mature. Others think smoking will help them feel more confident around others. It is important to choose friends who encourage you to make healthful choices, such as committing to be tobacco free.

It is **important** to choose friends who *encourage* you to make **healthful** choices.

It is also common for teens to start smoking when tobacco is used in their homes. Similar to peer pressure, families can pressure teens into using tobacco even if family members do not directly encourage smoking. For example, parents may warn against the dangers of tobacco use, but they may smoke. Having a sibling who smokes may also encourage tobacco use. Other reasons teens try tobacco include wanting to rebel, being curious, or thinking that the health risks do not apply to them.

⟩⟩⟩ Reading Check

DESCRIBE *Explain how teens are influenced by their peers to use tobacco.*

Tetra Images/Getty Images

Influence of the Media and Advertising

Another negative influence on teen smoking is the media. Although efforts have been made to reduce this influence, it is still common. Television shows, movies, and video games often show characters having fun while smoking. An estimated one-third of popular movies made for children and teens still show images of people smoking.

Tobacco companies spend millions of dollars to advertise their products. Colorful ads show happy, attractive people smoking. Nine out of ten smokers start smoking by age 18.

Here is what teens across the United States said in response to statements about tobacco use. *Evaluate how you would respond to these statements.*

Eighty percent of underage smokers use the three most-advertised brands. Tobacco companies see teens as a **target audience,** or *a group of people for which a product is intended.*

One key strategy tobacco companies use is **product placement,** which is *a paid arrangement a company has made to show its products in media such as television or film.* If you see a favorite celebrity smoking, it could have a strong influence on you. This would be especially true if you did not know how harmful tobacco products are to your health. Tobacco companies use another strategy to get shoppers' attention as they wait to pay for other items. **Point-of-sale promotions** are *advertising campaigns in which a product is promoted at a store's checkout counter.*

Refusing *Tobacco*

Sindhu and Andrea have been friends since the third grade. Now they are older and go to different schools. Andrea spends much of her time with her new friends. One day they meet after school, and Andrea offers Sindhu a cigarette. Sindhu wants to keep her friend, but she does not want to smoke. What should she say to Andrea? Remember the S.T.O.P. strategy:

* **S**ay no in a firm voice

* **T**ell why not.

* **O**ffer another idea.

* **P**romptly leave.

On Your Own
Role-play how Sindhu reacts when Andrea asks her to have a cigarette. How can Sindhu use the S.T.O.P. formula in this situation?

	Agree	Disagree	No Opinion or Do Not Know
Seeing someone smoke turns me off.	67%	22%	10%
I would only date people who don't smoke.	86%	8%	6%
It is safe to smoke for only a year or two.	7%	92%	1%
Smoking can help you when you're bored.	7%	92%	1%
Smoking helps reduce stress.	21%	78%	3%
Smoking helps keep your weight down.	18%	80%	2%
Chewing tobacco and snuff cause cancer.	95%	2%	3%
I strongly dislike being around smokers.	65%	22%	13%

Source: Centers for Disease Control and Prevention.

RESISTING TOBACCO USE

MAIN IDEA Knowing how to resist tobacco will help you stay tobacco free.

You can protect your health now and in the future if you make a commitment to stay tobacco free. If you make that choice, you will enjoy better physical, mental/emotional, and social health. Ninety percent of adult smokers start smoking before age 18. If you avoid tobacco use as a teen, you will greatly decrease the chance that you will smoke as an adult.

Reasons *to* Say No

Being tobacco free is a safe behavior that includes many benefits. A healthier body is just one of those benefits. Read the list below to learn more.

- **Overall health.** People who smoke get sick more easily and more often than nonsmokers.

- **Clear, healthy skin.** If you use tobacco, your skin cells are less able to take in oxygen and other important nutrients.
- **Fresh breath.** Cigarettes and smokeless tobacco products cause bad breath.
- **Clean, fresh-smelling clothes and hair.** Smokers usually smell like smoke. Stinky cigarette odors stick to clothes and hair and are not easy cleaned.
- **Better sports performance.** Nonsmokers are usually better athletes than smokers because they can breathe more deeply and are more healthy overall.
- **Money savings.** Tobacco is expensive. Increased taxes on tobacco mean the costs will keep going up. Teens who do not buy tobacco will have more to spend on other items such as clothes and music.

- **Environmental health.** By staying tobacco free, you help reduce secondhand smoke. You are also protecting the people around you.

Ways *to* Say No

You take responsibility for your health when you choose not to use tobacco. Choose to spend time with others who are tobacco free. Be prepared to be asked if you want to try tobacco. Practice your refusal skills to help you make the best decision. You can practice saying no in an assertive style that shows you are serious but also that you respect others. Speak in a firm voice with your head up. This will tell others you mean what you say.

Your Rights *as* a Nonsmoker

You have the right to breathe air that is free of tobacco smoke. Many laws are in place to protect nonsmokers. It has become easier to find smoke-free places. As a nonsmoker, you can ask people not to smoke around you.

> **>>> Reading Check**
>
> **GIVE EXAMPLES** *Identify three ways you can say no to tobacco.*

"I dislike the smell of smoke."

"I can't. I'm on the soccer team and need to keep my lungs in shape."

"My parents would ground me if they found out I was smoking."

"I can't afford to spend all my money on tobacco."

"Smoking is bad for you."

"It's against the law for someone my age to smoke."

"My grandfather had cancer. I don't want to go through what he did."

If someone offers you tobacco, here are some ways to say no. *Identify some other ways you can refuse tobacco.*

BREAKING THE TOBACCO HABIT

MAIN IDEA › Many resources are available to people who want to be tobacco free.

Some of the damage done by smoking can never be reversed. However, quitting tobacco does prevent more damage to the body and will improve a person's overall health. The process can be difficult, but there are many resources available.

Some of the **damage** done by *smoking* **can never be reversed.**

The body goes through physical changes when a person no longer uses tobacco. Learning to live without tobacco takes time and a lot of willpower. Tobacco users often try a variety of methods to try to quit before they find one that works for them.

Some people may choose to stop by going cold turkey, which means *stopping all use of tobacco products immediately.* The cold turkey method can be difficult for people because they need help breaking the addiction to nicotine. They will experience withdrawal symptoms for up to six months. One source of help is nicotine replacement therapies (NRTs), which are *products that assist a person in breaking a tobacco habit.* NRTs include nicotine gums, lozenges, and patches worn on the skin.

Many organizations also help users quit. For example, tobacco users can find tips and support groups through the American Lung Association, the American Heart Association, or the American Cancer Society. Some schools now have programs to help teens who want to quit using tobacco. If you know someone who is trying to get rid of a tobacco habit, you can share the following information:

- List your reasons.
- Get support and encouragement from family or friends.
- Set small goals.
- Choose tobacco-free places to spend time.
- Change your tobacco-related habits.
- Be physically active.
- Keep trying.

In addition to the types of health organizations noted above, other good sources of information for people who want to quit include hospitals, web sites, and libraries. Doctors and nurses can also be helpful in helping people quit tobacco use. Medical professionals can offer advice about ways to deal with the symptoms of nicotine withdrawal. Doctors may also prescribe certain NRTs for those unable to quit on their own.

>>> **Reading Check**

DEFINE *What are nicotine replacement therapies?* ■

>>> **After You Read**

1. **DEFINE** Explain what the term *cold turkey* means. Use it in a complete sentence.
2. **IDENTIFY** List at least three benefits of being tobacco free.
3. **SUMMARIZE** Explain how people who wish to stop using tobacco can get help.

>>> **Thinking Critically**

4. **INFER** Why is it easier never to start using tobacco than it is to quit once you have started?
5. **APPLY** How would you influence a peer to make the healthful choice to quit smoking?

>>> **Applying Health Skills**

6. **GOAL SETTING** Make a plan to help someone quit using tobacco. Research what resources are available online. Include alternative activities the tobacco user can do when he or she experiences the urge to use tobacco.

◷ Review

◀) Audio

Inside *Your* Lungs

WHAT YOU WILL NEED

* 64 sugar cubes
* Cellophane tape
* One sheet of graph paper

WHAT YOU WILL DO

1 Use the sugar cubes to make a square that is 4 cubes long, 4 wide, and 4 deep.

2 Use tape to hold the sugar cubes together.

3 Use the graph paper to figure out how many paper squares can be covered by the large sugar rectangle.

4 Remove the tape and measure how many paper squares can be covered by a single cube. Remember to record all six sides.

5 Multiply this single cube measurement by 64.

WRAPPING IT UP

Which covers more graph paper squares: the large sugar rectangle or the 64 cubes? The cubes represent your alveoli. Just breathing in does not get oxygen to your body cells. It only gets it to your lungs. Alveoli pass oxygen to your blood. Dividing the lungs into many smaller sacs (alveoli) gets more oxygen to your blood faster. Warm-blooded animals like us need this trick. We need to get oxygen at a fast enough rate to perform all our activities.

You've learned that smoking affects your lungs. Do you remember what's inside your lungs? Each lung contains millions of little sacs called alveoli. When you inhale, oxygen and anything else you breathe makes its way into these 600 million little sacs. Blood vessels surround the alveoli. They pick up oxygen from the alveoli and carry it to your cells. Smoking makes the alveoli less able to handle the oxygen your body needs.

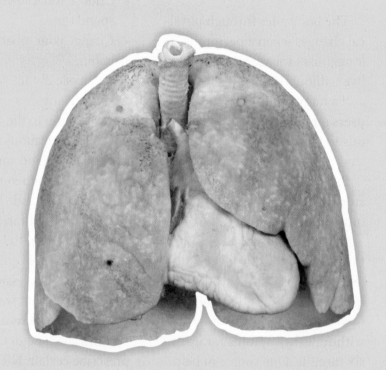

READING REVIEW

FOLDABLES and Other Study Aids

Take out the Foldable® that you created for Lesson 1 and any study organizers that you created for Lessons 2–5. Find a partner and quiz each other using these study aids.

LESSON 1 Facts About Tobacco

BIG IDEA The substances contained in tobacco products are very harmful to your health.

* Tobacco is a harmful and addictive substance in all its forms—cigarettes, cigars and pipes, and smokeless.
* Tobacco contains many chemicals that can harm your body, including nicotine, tar, and carbon monoxide.

LESSON 2 Health Risks of Tobacco Use

BIG IDEA Tobacco is a dangerous drug with serious health consequences.

* Health experts have been warning about the dangers of tobacco for many years.
* Tobacco use causes many serious health problems, such as emphysema, lung cancer, and heart disease.

LESSON 3 Tobacco Addiction

BIG IDEA Tobacco contains nicotine, which is an extremely powerful and addictive drug.

* Tobacco contains strong substances that make it difficult to stop using once a person has started.
* Tobacco use results in both physical and psychological dependence on nicotine.

LESSON 4 Costs to Society

BIG IDEA Tobacco has consequences in addition to the harm it causes tobacco users.

* Tobacco use is costly not only to smokers but also to nonsmokers.
* Added health care expenses and lost productivity are major costs to society as a result of tobacco use.
* Laws and education help protect nonsmokers and lower the cost of tobacco use to society.
* Efforts to counter the costs of tobacco use include tobacco taxes, smoke-free environments, labeling laws, and advertising limits.

LESSON 5 Saying No to Tobacco Use

BIG IDEA It is important to have strategies to resist the strong influences around tobacco use.

* Influences that can lead teens to try tobacco may come from peers, family, the media, and advertising.
* Knowing how to resist tobacco, including the reasons to say no, will help you stay tobacco free.
* Resources available to people who want to be tobacco free include certain medical products along with various organizations and support groups.

 Review

 Web Quest

ASSESSMENT

Reviewing Vocabulary *and* Main Ideas

- › physical dependence
- › withdrawal
- › nicotine
- › lungs
- › smokeless tobacco
- › carbon monoxide
- › addiction
- › cardiovascular
- › emphysema

» On a sheet of paper, write the numbers 1–9. After each number, write the term from the list that best completes each statement.

LESSON 1 Facts About Tobacco

1. _____ is an addictive drug found in tobacco leaves and in all tobacco products.

2. A poisonous, odorless gas found in tobacco smoke is _____.

3. _____ is ground tobacco that is chewed or inhaled through the nose.

LESSON 2 Health Risks of Tobacco Use

4. Tobacco smoke damages the air sacs in the lungs, which can cause _____.

5. Tobacco use affects the circulatory or _____ system, which includes the heart and blood vessels.

6. Cancer of the _____ is the leading cause of death among people who smoke.

LESSON 3 Tobacco Addiction

7. Anyone who stops using tobacco goes through nicotine _____.

8. Nicotine is a powerful drug that causes _____.

9. _____ on nicotine involves the body developing a chemical need for the drug.

» On a sheet of paper, write the numbers 10–15. Write *True* or *False* for each statement below. If the statement is false, change the underlined word or phrase to make it true.

LESSON 4 Costs to Society

10. Whenever people smoke near you, you breathe their <u>secondhand smoke</u>, or environmental tobacco smoke (ETS).

11. Many state and local governments have tried to lower the cost to nonsmokers through laws that <u>require</u> smoking in all public spaces.

12. Tobacco products are required to carry clear labels or disclaimers saying that smoking is <u>healthful</u>.

LESSON 5 Saying No to Tobacco Use

13. <u>Peer pressure</u> can help you say no if you are pressured to try tobacco.

14. Some people may choose to stop using tobacco suddenly and completely, or by going <u>cold turkey</u>.

15. Ninety percent of adult smokers start smoking <u>after</u> age 18.

✔ eAssessment

>> Using complete sentences, answer the following questions on a sheet of paper.

☁️ *Thinking* **Critically**

16. APPLY Nadine smells tobacco on her sister Shari's hair and clothes one afternoon. How could Nadine talk to her sister about the tobacco smell without accusing her of smoking?

17. SYNTHESIZE Explain how someone becomes addicted to tobacco. Include facts about addiction and a description of the path to addiction.

● *Write* **About It**

18. PERSONAL WRITING Write a story about a teen who is faced with a difficult decision. The teen has to decide whether to join a club in which the members smoke and use other tobacco products. Use the six steps of the decision-making process to show how the teen makes a healthful choice.

Ⓐ Ⓑ
Ⓒ Ⓓ **STANDARDIZED TEST PRACTICE**

Math
Use the directions and chart below to answer the questions on the right.

In order to run the marathon, Melissa knows she needs to stay tobacco free. To qualify for the race, she needs to improve the time it takes her to run one mile. She tracks her time on a weekly basis. Refer to the chart below to see Melissa's progress.

Week	Time to run 1 mile (min)
1	16
2	11
3	9
4	8

1. By what percent did Melissa improve her time from Week 2 to Week 3?
  A. 15%
  B. 18%
  C. 20%
  D. 23%

2. During which time did Melissa show a 50 percent improvement?
  A. From Week 1 to Week 2
  B. From Week 1 to Week 4
  C. From Week 2 to Week 4
  D. From Week 3 to Week 4

Alcohol

LESSONS

PREMIUM ONLINE RESOURCES

 Audio
 Videos
Bilingual Glossary

Fitness Zone
Web Quest
Review

Using alcohol as a teen can have serious consequences. *What are some of the risks associated with using alcohol?*

Alcohol Use *and* Teens

BIG IDEA Most teens do not use alcohol, but several factors influence teens to try it.

Before You Read

QUICK WRITE Write a few sentences describing what you already know about alcohol use.

▶ Video

As You Read

 Study Organizer

Make the Foldable to record the information presented in the Lesson.

Vocabulary

> alcohol
> drug
> depressant
> inhibitions
> binge drinking
> minor

🔊 Audio

🔤 Bilingual Glossary

Developing Good Character

Respect Choosing to be alcohol free shows that you respect yourself. Create, sign, and date a pledge listing your reasons for choosing to avoid alcohol. Remember that this pledge is a promise to yourself to make a healthful choice. *Identify a way you could encourage your peers to also make healthful choices regarding alcohol.*

WHAT IS ALCOHOL?

MAIN IDEA Alcohol is a drug that affects the mind and body.

Have you seen spoiled food that has mold growing on it? This change is caused by a chemical reaction. Alcohol is *a drug created by a chemical reaction in some foods, especially fruits and grains.* The type of alcohol in beer, wine, and liquor is one of the most widely used and abused drugs in the United States.

Over time, using too much alcohol can damage body organs and cause disease. Alcohol also affects the brain and central nervous system, causing changes in behavior. Alcohol is considered a drug, or *a substance other than food that changes the structure or function of the body or mind.*

Alcohol acts as a depressant, or *a drug that slows down the body's functions and reactions, including heart and breathing rates.* These physical changes may make it difficult to think and act responsibly.

> Using **too much** *alcohol* can **damage** body organs and cause **disease.**

Not all alcohol use is bad. For adults, a small amount of wine each day may help keep the cardiovascular system healthy. However, that amount is limited to one 5 oz. glass of wine per day for an adult female and two glasses for an adult male. For some people, though, even small amounts of alcohol can affect how they feel and behave.

Alcohol use can cause people to lose their inhibitions, meaning they have no *conscious or unconscious restraint on their behaviors or actions.* Some people may act in ways that are not typical for that person. Some people become relaxed and friendly. Others become depressed and angry. Under the influence of alcohol, people often say and do things they will later regret.

WHY DO SOME TEENS USE ALCOHOL?

MAIN IDEA Teens face many influences that encourage them to try alcohol.

Studies show that most teens do not use alcohol. So why do some teens try it, even when they know alcohol is harmful to their health and also illegal? Curiosity is one reason a teen may try alcohol. Another reason is that they think it will make them more popular. Some teens think alcohol use makes them feel relaxed or more grown up. Others use it to feel some relief from emotions that they have not yet learned how to handle.

Alcohol *in the* Media

Television commercials, movies, Internet sites, and online ads often make using alcohol seem fun and exciting. You have probably seen an ad for some type of alcoholic drink. The people who appear in the ads look young and attractive. Companies that make and sell alcohol do this on purpose. They don't want people to see or think about the negative effects of their products.

Media images may lead some teens to feel that drinking alcohol is okay. Some teens may also think that using alcohol will add more fun and excitement to their lives, like the people in the ads.

> ### Reading Check
> **CHARACTERIZE** *What are some typical reasons that a teen may try alcohol?*

Peer Pressure

"I want to be cool, too." That's a thought many teens often have before they try alcohol, even though they may not really want to. Negative peer pressure is another major reason why some teens use alcohol. Some may choose to use alcohol to try to fit in or to not be embarrassed in front of their friends.

However, having even one drink can be harmful to your health. Simply trying alcohol can lead to risky situations. For example, sometimes teens may dare one another to consume a lot of alcohol very quickly. *Having several drinks in a short period of time,* or binge drinking, is very dangerous and can even cause death. It is not always easy to say no, but negative peer pressure is not a good reason to choose alcohol.

Even *one drink* can be **harmful** to *your* health.

Media ads are designed to make products look fun and exciting. *What elements of alcohol ads might encourage a teen to try alcohol?*

Huntstock/Getty Images

REASONS NOT TO DRINK

MAIN IDEA ⟩ The negative effects of alcohol use pose even greater risks for teens.

The USDA recommends that adults who choose to use alcohol consume it only in moderation. This is defined as no more than one drink per day for an adult female and no more than two for an adult male. However, some people should never consume alcohol. According to the CDC, those who should not use alcohol at all include people who are:

- **Minors,** or *people under the age of adult rights and responsibilities.* For alcohol, a minor is anyone younger than age 21.
- Pregnant or women who are trying to become pregnant.

- Taking medications that can be harmful when they are mixed with alcohol.
- Recovering from alcoholism or unable to control the amount they drink.
- Facing any type of medical condition that can be made worse by alcohol use.
- Driving, planning to drive, or engaging in any other activity that requires skill, coordination, and alertness.

The use of alcohol can have harmful effects for anyone, but teens are especially at risk. During the teen years, your body is still growing and developing.

When teens consume alcohol, their bodies do not grow and develop properly. Alcohol can seriously harm the brain's ability to learn and remember.

Teens also face many emotional changes. They might think that alcohol can help them better deal with their emotions. However, alcohol can make a teen's social and emotional life more difficult. Many people who use alcohol feel bad about themselves. They may have a hard time making friends and relating to others. Alcohol use can disrupt sleep and create more stress than it may seem to relieve.

Health SKILLS ACTIVITY

Stress Management

Dealing with *Emotions*

Dealing with difficult emotions is part of life for a teen. Rather than using alcohol, teens can use the following strategies to deal with emotions in healthful ways.

* Get enough sleep. Being well-rested can give you the energy you need to deal with difficult feelings and stress.

* Take some deep breaths. This can help you relax.

* Stay active. Physical activity can help you focus your energy and lower your stress level.

* Talk to someone you trust and respect about what you're feeling.

On Your Own

Work with a group to create a brochure or blog post for your fellow classmates that describes positive ways to deal with difficult emotions. Be sure to point out the negative effects of using alcohol to deal with difficult emotions.

Teens who consume alcohol also risk trouble with the law. It is illegal for a minor to use alcohol. Buying or drinking alcohol can lead to an arrest, a fine, or time in a youth detention center. A person of any age who is convicted of driving while intoxicated (DWI), or driving under the influence (DUI), risks losing his or her license. If that person causes an accident and someone is injured, the driver may face more serious consequences.

Teens who use *alcohol* also risk **legal trouble.**

Choosing not to use alcohol is a healthful decision. It shows that you understand how risky alcohol use can be. As you have learned, some teens may believe that using alcohol will help them fit in with their peers. In reality, most teens do not use alcohol. By choosing not to drink, you will already be fitting in with most people your age. Many teens realize the negative effects that alcohol can have on all sides of their health triangle and are saying no to alcohol use.

>>> **Reading Check**

DEFINE *What is a minor? How does this term relate to alcohol?* ■

Many teens are making the decision to stay alcohol free. *Explain how abstaining from alcohol can improve your health.*

©Creatas/PunchStock

>>> **After You Read**

1. **VOCABULARY** Define alcohol. Use it in a sentence.
2. **EXPLAIN** What are two reasons teens often give for using alcohol?
3. **STATE** What are two reasons not to drink alcohol?

>>> **Thinking Critically**

4. **APPLY** What do you think is the most important reason for a teen not to use alcohol?
5. **PREDICT** How can using alcohol affect a teen's development?

>>> **Applying Health Skills**

6. **ACCESSING INFORMATION** Some teens may believe myths about alcohol. With classmates, research several of these myths. Use your findings to create a poster showing the truth about these concepts.

🔄 Review

🔊 Audio

Effects *of* Alcohol Use

BIG IDEA Alcohol use has far-reaching effects to the body, other people, and personal relationships.

Before You Read

QUICK WRITE Write a few sentences describing what you already know about the harmful effects of alcohol.

▶ Video

As You Read

STUDY ORGANIZER Make the study organizer on page 87 to record the information presented in Lesson 2.

Vocabulary

› intoxicated
› blood alcohol concentration (BAC)
› alcohol poisoning
› ulcer
› fatty liver
› cirrhosis
› reaction time
› fetal alcohol syndrome (FAS)

🔊 Audio

🔤 Bilingual Glossary

HOW ALCOHOL AFFECTS THE BODY

MAIN IDEA Alcohol has many short- and long-term effects on your body.

Alcohol begins to affect body systems soon after it is consumed. It is quickly absorbed by the bloodstream. Alcohol affects the brain and central nervous system as soon as 30 seconds after it is consumed. Alcohol does not affect everyone in the same way, however. Some people can consume more than others before they become intoxicated.

Intoxicated means *physically and mentally impaired by the use of alcohol.* In other words, it means "having consumed more alcohol than the body can tolerate." This is also known as "being drunk." However, the amount of alcohol someone consumes is only one factor in understanding the effects of alcohol use.

How Alcohol's Effects Vary

Different people react to alcohol use in different ways. One of the biggest factors is the user's blood alcohol concentration (BAC). This is *the amount of alcohol in the blood.* An alcohol user's BAC is expressed as a percentage.

Alcohol begins to **affect** body systems *soon* after it is consumed.

A blood alcohol concentration of 0.02 percent will cause most people to feel light-headed. A BAC of 0.08 percent interferes with a person's ability to drive a car safely. Police officers use this percentage to determine whether a person is legally intoxicated. A BAC of 0.40 percent can lead to coma and death. A number of other factors can also influence how alcohol affects an individual. A person's size and gender make a difference. So does how much alcohol someone consumes and how fast.

Developing Good Character

Being a Responsible Friend One way of showing you are responsible is by looking out for the well-being of others. Don't let a friend get in a car with a driver who has been drinking. If a friend is using alcohol, urge that person to get help. Don't hesitate to talk to an adult if your friend is unwilling to seek help. This is not breaking your friend's trust. It is taking the first step in getting your friend the help that he or she needs. *Cite another example of showing responsibility in dealing with substance abuse.*

SHORT-TERM EFFECTS

MAIN IDEA The use of alcohol has an immediate effect on many parts of the body.

Alcohol has both short-term and long-term effects on the body. The use of alcohol not only causes immediate risks, but it can also cause serious health problems over time. Alcohol can affect the brain, stomach, liver, and kidneys right away. Using a lot of alcohol over time can cause serious damage to these organs.

The use of *alcohol* can cause **serious** health problems.

ALCOHOL AND THE BRAIN
Alcohol is absorbed into the bloodstream and reaches the brain very quickly. As a result, the brain and nervous system slow down immediately. Even one drink can make it difficult to think clearly. Alcohol blocks messages trying to get to the brain. After more drinks, it becomes harder to concentrate and remember. Also, it becomes difficult to speak clearly or walk in a straight line. People under the influence of alcohol may also feel dizzy, have blurred vision, and lose their balance. A person under the influence of alcohol is also more likely to engage in other risk behaviors such as driving while intoxicated, tobacco and other drug use, sexual activity, and acts of violence.

ALCOHOL AND THE STOMACH
In the stomach, alcohol increases the flow of acid used for digestion. Some people become sick to their stomach. Most of the alcohol passes into the small intestine. Some, however, is absorbed into the bloodstream and causes the blood vessels to expand. From the bloodstream, alcohol passes into the liver.

Beer 12 oz. **Wine** 5 oz. **Liquor** 1.5 oz.

Each of the drinks shown contains the same amount of alcohol. *How much beer would a person need to drink to consume the same amount of alcohol as in two glasses of wine?*

ALCOHOL AND THE HEART
Alcohol affects the way the heart pumps blood through the body. Because it makes the blood vessels wider, the blood comes closer to the surface of the skin. This makes a person who is consuming alcohol feel warm, but his or her body temperature is actually dropping. Alcohol also slows down a person's heart rate.

ALCOHOL AND THE LIVER AND KIDNEYS
Short-term use of alcohol also affects the liver and kidneys. The liver acts like a filter, taking alcohol from the bloodstream and removing it from the body. However, the liver can filter only about half an ounce of alcohol from the bloodstream each hour. Any additional alcohol that is consumed stays in the bloodstream and affects the body. In addition, alcohol causes the kidneys to produce more urine. Extra urine production can lead to dehydration, or the loss of important body fluids. When people consume too much alcohol, they often feel more thirsty than usual the next day.

ALCOHOL POISONING
If someone consumes a lot of alcohol very quickly, it can lead to alcohol poisoning. This is *a dangerous condition that results when a person drinks excessive amounts of alcohol over a short time period.* Binge drinking is a common cause of alcohol poisoning. A person who has too much too quickly may vomit, become unconscious, or have trouble breathing. Alcohol poisoning can result in death.

>>> **Reading Check**
IDENTIFY *Which parts of the body are affected by alcohol?*

LONG-TERM EFFECTS

MAIN IDEA Alcohol use affects all areas of a person's life.

Consuming alcohol regularly can lead to a number of serious health problems. Alcohol use can damage major organs and make existing health problems worse. It can also lead to learning and memory problems.

BRAIN Alcohol affects the parts of the brain which control memory and problem solving. Alcohol also destroys brain cells. Because brain cells do not grow back, this can be serious enough to limit everyday functions. Alcohol can also block messages sent to the brain. When this happens, people can have a hard time seeing, hearing, or moving.

HEART Heavy drinking makes the heart weak and enlarged, which leads to high blood pressure. The risk of congestive heart failure and stroke also increases with excessive alcohol use.

STOMACH Alcohol causes your body to create more acid. Stomach acid usually helps with digestion. However, the extra acid created by alcohol consumption can eventually cause sores called ulcers to develop in the stomach lining. An ulcer is *an open sore in the stomach lining.* Drinking alcohol also makes the valve between your stomach and esophagus weak. This valve usually works to keeps acid in the stomach. When it is weakened by alcohol use, acid comes up and causes heartburn.

Alcohol use can **damage** major **organs** and make existing *health* **problems** **even worse.**

LIVER Consuming alcohol regularly over a long period of time puts a serious strain on the liver. Fatty liver is *a condition in which fats build up in the liver and cannot be broken down.* Heavy drinkers are particularly at risk of developing cirrhosis, or *the scarring and destruction of liver tissue.* This condition can be deadly. Cirrhosis creates scar tissue that prevents blood from flowing normally through the liver. If the liver is not working correctly, it cannot filter out wastes or remove other poisons from the blood. These poisons can eventually reach the brain and cause more damage.

>>> **Reading Check**

ANALYZE *Which of the effects of alcohol use do you feel would have the most serious impact on your health? Explain your answer.*

OTHER DANGERS OF ALCOHOL USE

MAIN IDEA Alcohol use can affect thoughts and behavior.

Because alcohol affects the brain, it also affects thoughts and behaviors. As a result, a person who consumes alcohol can cause arguments, physical fights, and vehicle accidents. The person may engage in risky behavior, such as using illegal drugs or engaging in sexual activity.

Alcohol *and* Driving

A person who uses alcohol experiences loss of coordination, concentration, and visual awareness. He or she also has slowed reaction time, or *the ability of the body to respond quickly and appropriately to situations.* Driving while intoxicated is extremely dangerous for the driver, his or her passengers, and others on the road. It is very important for your safety not to ride in a vehicle with a driver who has been using alcohol. If a person has been drinking, do your best to avoid letting them drive. You can always call someone else to come pick you up.

Alcohol *and* Behavior

Using alcohol can also damage your mental/emotional and social health. Teens who use alcohol are more likely to do poorly in school. A teen who uses alcohol may start to lose interest in his or her favorite activities. In addition, that person may risk losing friends as a result of his or her alcohol use.

Someone under the influence of alcohol might also engage in other risk behaviors such as tobacco use or sexual activity. Alcohol use can lead a person to make unhealthful decisions.

It is very **important** for your safety *not to ride* in a vehicle with a **driver** who has been **using alcohol.**

Alcohol *and* Pregnancy

If a pregnant woman consumes alcohol, it passes through her bloodstream to her baby. This can lead to what is known as fetal alcohol syndrome (FAS), or *alcohol-related birth defects that include both physical and mental problems.* A baby born with fetal alcohol syndrome can have low birth weight and a smaller-than-normal brain. FAS can also cause serious heart and kidney problems. As they grow older, babies who were born with FAS may also develop speech problems and have learning disabilities.

>>> **Reading Check**

INFER *Why does slowed reaction time make driving while intoxicated so dangerous?* ■

LESSON 2

REVIEW

>>>**After You Read**

1. **DESCRIBE** What kinds of long-term damage can alcohol use cause?
2. **RECALL** Describe how alcohol affects the mind.
3. **VOCABULARY** Define blood alcohol content. Use the term in a sentence.

>>>**Thinking Critically**

4. **APPLY** You are at a park with friends. When it is time to leave, a friend's brother offers you a ride. You smell alcohol on his breath. What should you do, and why?
5. **ANALYZE** Why is a person under the influence of alcohol more likely to engage in other high-risk behaviors?

>>>**Applying Health Skills**

6. **ACCESSING INFORMATION** Some teens may believe myths about alcohol. With classmates, research several of these myths. Use your findings to create a poster showing the truth about these concepts.

 Review

Audio

Alcoholism *and* Alcohol Abuse

BIG IDEA Alcohol is a highly addictive drug that can lead to disease and damage relationships.

Before You Read

QUICK WRITE Make a list of the reasons you can think of to avoid alcohol use.

▶ Video

As You Read

STUDY ORGANIZER Make the study organizer on page 87 to record the information presented in Lesson 3.

Vocabulary

› alcoholism
› malnutrition
› alcohol abuse
› substance abuse

🔊 Audio

🔤 Bilingual Glossary

🏃 Fitness Zone

Stress-relieving activities Some people use alcohol to relieve stress. I think of other ways to deal with my stress. I can write a list of things I like to do that help me get rid of stress and stay healthy: run, play basketball, read a book, have a healthful snack with my mom, or ride my bike.

ALCOHOL'S ADDICTIVE POWER

MAIN IDEA Alcohol is a powerful drug that can cause addiction.

One of the greatest dangers with alcohol use is that it is habit-forming. As with other drugs, using alcohol regularly can lead to addiction. Teens age 15 and younger are four times more likely to become addicted than older people. A person who uses alcohol in large amounts is even more likely to become addicted. An addiction to any drug can change a person's life. It takes the focus off healthful goals. It can also damage relationships with family and friends.

Alcohol use is a serious health issue. Estimates show that at least 17 million people in the U.S. have an alcohol problem. Alcohol addiction has a negative impact on that person's entire life. Alcohol addiction affects all three sides of a user's health triangle—physical, mental/emotional, and social.

> One of the **greatest dangers** with *alcohol use* is that it is **habit-forming.**

How can someone tell if a person has an alcohol problem? A person who is addicted to alcohol frequently uses it alone. He or she often uses alcohol to the point of becoming intoxicated. Using this drug typically becomes more important than anything else in a person's life. Someone with an alcohol problem may ignore friends or lose them entirely. That person often neglects his or her family. Many people who are addicted to alcohol do poorly in school or at work. They may lose their jobs or get in trouble with the law. Most people with an alcohol problem need to use it every day in order to function. Some may even forget to eat regularly and stop taking care of themselves.

THE DISEASE OF ALCOHOLISM

MAIN IDEA The disease of alcoholism results from addiction and has physical, mental/emotional, and social consequences.

People who are addicted to alcohol suffer from alcoholism, or *a disease in which a person has a physical and psychological need for alcohol.* They are called *alcoholics.* Alcoholics typically experience some or all of the following symptoms of alcoholism:

- **Craving** is a strong feeling of need to consume alcohol. This is likely related to alcohol's effects on the brain.
- **Loss of control** means the user is unable to limit his or her alcohol consumption.
- **Tolerance** is when your body needs more and more of a drug to get the same effect. If someone is an alcoholic, he or she will need to consume more and more alcohol in order to feel intoxicated.
- **Physical dependence** can lead to painful symptoms. If an alcoholic stops using alcohol, he or she may experience sweating, shaking, or anxiety. Making excuses to drink is another common symptom. An alcoholic may be unable to limit how much he or she consumes at one time. Alcoholism may also cause a person to become irritable or violent. This can result in injury or abuse. Alcoholics may hurt themselves or others.

>>> **Reading Check**

IDENTIFY *What makes alcohol such a dangerous drug?*

Making excuses to **drink** is another common **symptom** of *alcoholism.*

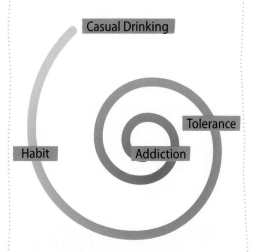

Casual Drinking

Tolerance

Habit

Addiction

The spiral of addiction begins with casual alcohol use. *Draw a conclusion about where the spiral ends.*

Stages *of* Alcoholism

Alcoholism is a disease that develops over time. The cycle of addiction is sometimes represented by a downward spiral. The spiral in the figure above shows how addiction to alcohol starts and progresses along the way. Alcohol addiction typically starts with casual drinking. After a person starts using alcohol casually, it can then become a habit. Once alcohol use is a habit, the body builds up a tolerance, which spirals toward addiction.

Each of the three stages of alcoholism may be either long or short. How long each stage goes on depends on the individual and on how old he or she is when the alcohol use begins. All alcoholics do not go through each stage in the same way.

- **Stage One—Abuse.** The user may have short-term memory loss and blackouts. He or she may also begin to lie or make excuses for drinking. It is also common for a person who abuses alcohol to begin saying or doing hurtful things to friends and family members.
- **Stage Two—Dependence.** The alcoholic loses control and cannot stop drinking. The person's body begins to depend on the drug. The user can become aggressive, avoid family and friends, or have physical problems. The user typically tries to hide his or her alcohol problem but is unable to function well at home, school, or work.
- **Stage Three—Addiction.** The person may be intoxicated for long periods of time. The liver may already be damaged. Less alcohol may be needed to cause intoxication. Common at this stage are strange fears, hallucinations, and malnutrition. This is *a condition in which the body does not get the nutrients it needs to grow and function properly.*

Helping a *Friend*

Mariah and Jenelle have been best friends for a long time. Mariah recently told Jenelle that her mom drinks alcohol nearly every day and sometimes becomes violent. Mariah also said that sometimes she gets very scared. Jenelle wonders what she should do to help Mariah.

What Would You Do?

Apply the six steps of the decision-making process to Mariah's situation.

1. State the situation.
2. List the options.
3. Weigh the possible outcomes.
4. Consider your values.
5. Make a decision and act on it.
6. Evaluate the decision.

With a partner, role-play what Jenelle would say to Mariah and how Mariah might respond.

How Alcoholism Affects Families

Alcoholism is a problem that affects more people than just the alcoholic. It can be a painful experience for family members as well. Children of alcoholics sometimes blame themselves, thinking they did something to drive a parent to alcohol. This is not the case. A child is never to blame for a parent's alcoholism.

Denial is also a problem for family and friends. Often, they do not want to admit that a loved one has an addiction. Family members may focus on helping the alcoholic and not take care of their own needs.

> Using alcohol can lead to unhealthy relationships. *Describe some ways that addiction can cause problems in relationships.*

If the alcoholic is abusive, this can have a negative effect. Friends may try to help by making an alcoholic feel comfortable with his or her behavior. This only encourages the addiction. It can create an unhealthy pattern and keep the alcoholic from getting the help he or she needs.

How Alcoholism Affects Society

Teen alcohol use costs the U.S. more than $50 billion a year. The total cost of alcohol-related problems is estimated at $223.5 billion a year. That figure is higher than the total for smoking and other drug-related issues. The greatest impact is on health care, law enforcement, and the workplace. Doctors and nurses have to take care of people with alcohol problems. Police and the courts must deal with people who break alcohol laws. A business can lose money when an employee who uses alcohol does not work hard on the job.

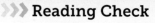

>>> Reading Check

DETERMINE *Where does the cycle of addiction usually begin?*

Avoiding alcohol makes it easier to focus in school. *Explain how alcohol abuse can make it hard to concentrate.*

©OJO Images Ltd/Alamy

ALCOHOL ABUSE

MAIN IDEA Alcohol abuse is different than alcoholism.

Although the terms *alcoholism* and *alcohol abuse* are sometimes used in the same way, there is a difference. Alcohol abuse means *using alcohol in ways that are unhealthy, illegal, or both.* People who abuse alcohol are not physically dependent on the drug. Their bodies are not in extreme need for the drug.

Alcohol abuse is different than alcoholism.

Alcohol abuse is a type of substance abuse, which involves *using illegal or harmful drugs, including any use of alcohol while under the legal drinking age.*

Alcohol abuse has four main symptoms. These include:

- Failing to complete major work tasks or ignoring responsibilities at home or school.
- Drinking in situations that are dangerous. For example, driving when intoxicated or riding with someone who has been drinking can result in an accident and serious injury.
- Having ongoing financial or legal problems.
- Continuing to drink even after the person has a problem with a friend or family member.

>>> **Reading Check**

IDENTIFY *Name a behavior that may occur when someone abuses alcohol.* ■

>>> **After You Read**

1. **VOCABULARY** Define alcohol abuse. Use the term in a complete sentence.
2. **EXPLAIN** What is the difference between alcoholism and alcohol abuse?
3. **DESCRIBE** Briefly describe the spiral of addiction.

>>> **Thinking Critically**

4. **ANALYZE** Layla has started drinking alcohol. Now she is forgetting things and lying to others about her alcohol use. She also has been in more arguments with her friends and family. What stage of alcoholism is Layla likely experiencing?
5. **EVALUATE** Briefly explain why alcohol use is even more dangerous for teens.

>>> **Applying Health Skills**

6. **DECISION MAKING** A friend has been irritable and moody lately. He tells you that he really needs alcohol and asks you to help him get some. He thinks only alcohol will make him feel better. Use the decision-making steps to make a responsible choice.

 Review

 Audio

Getting Help *for* Alcohol Abuse

BIG IDEA Many resources are available to help alcoholics, alcohol abusers, and their families.

Before You Read

QUICK WRITE Name a person you might turn to when you need help with a problem. Write a brief description of this person's qualities, such as being a good listener

 Video

As You Read

STUDY ORGANIZER Make the study organizer on page 87 to record the information presented in Lesson 4.

Vocabulary

> enablers
> intervention
> recovery
> detoxification

 Audio

🔤 Bilingual Glossary

Developing Good Character

Citizenship Students Against Destructive Decisions (SADD) helps people understand the harmful effects of alcohol on teens. Do some research on SADD. Find out how you and your classmates can get involved with this organization. Discuss your findings with your class.

HELP FOR ALCOHOL ABUSE

MAIN IDEA Family, friends, and organizations can all help someone with an alcohol problem.

People who are struggling with alcohol need help. However, many cannot admit they have a problem. Sometimes alcoholics surround themselves with enablers. These are *persons who create an atmosphere in which the alcoholic can comfortably continue his or her unacceptable behavior.* Enabling may allow an alcoholic to continue drinking without facing any negative consequences. A way to overcome this situation is to hold an **intervention,** or *a gathering where family and friends get a problem drinker to agree to seek help.* During an intervention, an alcoholic's family and friends can discuss their concerns about the alcohol abuse. They can try to convince the abuser to stop using alcohol. An intervention may include commitments by friends and family to no longer enable the alcoholic's behavior.

Before holding an intervention, family members and friends may choose to meet with a substance abuse counselor. A counselor can often make arrangements for the alcoholic to get treatment. Friends and family members can then use the intervention to encourage the person with the alcohol problem to seek help.

Ways *to* Seek Help

Groups such as Alcoholics Anonymous (AA) can help people who are addicted to alcohol. Similar groups help friends and families of alcoholics. Support groups work to help people break their patterns of addiction. They allow people to talk with others who are facing the same problem. You can search online to learn more about these groups.

People who are *struggling* with **alcohol** need **help.**

The Road *to* Recovery

Before an alcoholic can get better, he or she must decide never to drink again. When that happens, **recovery,** or *the process of learning to live an alcohol-free life,* can begin. As we have learned, addiction is very powerful. Recovery is usually long and difficult. It involves several steps that each person must follow.

- **Admission.** The person must first admit that he or she has an addiction and ask for help.
- **Detoxification,** or *the physical process of freeing the body of an addictive substance.* Detoxification marks only the beginning of breaking the physical addiction. An alcoholic may go through withdrawal when he or she suddenly stops using alcohol.
- **Counseling.** Alcoholics need outside help from counselors and support groups to recover. As we have learned, there are local organizations that can help provide a support group.

- **Resolution.** The alcoholic commits to accepting responsibility for his or her actions. After recovery, people who have had alcohol problems are called recovering alcoholics. A recovering alcoholic is someone who has an addiction to alcohol but chooses to live without alcohol.

Even after a person goes through recovery, he or she must always fight addiction. Recovery is never final. Recovering alcoholics risk a relapse if they drink again. That is why it is important they decide to always make wise choices related to alcohol.

⟩⟩⟩ Reading Check

EXPLAIN *What makes recovery from alcoholism so difficult?*

A recovering alcoholic must always fight the addiction. *Give examples of some healthful choices that would help someone remain alcohol free.*

Health SKILLS ACTIVITY

Communication Skills

When *Communication* Counts Most

Y ou may be able to help a friend or family member who has an alcohol problem. Here's how.

* **HAVE AN HONEST TALK.** Find a time when the person is sober. Discuss your concerns, and talk about the effects alcohol can have on a person's health.

* **ENCOURAGE THE PERSON TO SEEK HELP.** After expressing your concerns, explain why he or she needs help and support.

* **OFFER INFORMATION.** Provide details about where the person can go for help. Make sure the person understands what help is available and how to get it.

With A Group Role-play a conversation in which you use the skills outlined above. Think about specific words that would express your concern and encourage the person to get help.

HELP FOR FAMILIES

MAIN IDEA Support groups can help families of alcoholics.

Families and friends of alcoholics can get help too. For example, Al-Anon teaches about the effects of alcoholism. This group also helps people learn strategies for dealing with an alcoholic.

Alateen helps teens who have parents who abuse alcohol. Organizations like these may offer group sessions or direct families to counseling and mental health resources. Al-Anon and Alateen also help educate the public.

>>> **Reading Check**

IDENTIFY *Name one example of a support group for families of alcohol abusers.*

This support group was formed to help families of people who suffer from alcoholism. *What are some support groups for alcoholism in your area?*

STAYING ALCOHOL FREE

MAIN IDEA Choosing not to use alcohol is the best way to avoid its dangers.

As you have learned, the use of alcohol has serious physical, mental/emotional, and social consequences. Choosing to be alcohol free is the best way not to experience these dangers. You can try to avoid situations where people are drinking alcohol. If someone pressures you to drink alcohol, use refusal skills.

Practice the S.T.O.P. strategy:
- **S**ay no in a firm voice.
- **T**ell why not.
- **O**ffer another idea.
- **P**romptly leave.

If you choose friends who are also alcohol free, you will have a support system. When you are around people who make healthful choices, it is easier for you to make healthful choices.

Positive peer pressure can make it more likely that you and your friends will choose activities that do not involve alcohol.

Choosing **not to use alcohol** is the best way to *avoid its dangers.*

Colleen Cahill/VIBE/Alamy

Benefits *of* Staying Alcohol Free

Staying alcohol free is a choice to lead a healthy lifestyle. When you choose not to use alcohol, you are showing respect for yourself and your body. You are choosing to remain in control of who you are.

Staying **alcohol free** is a *choice* to lead a **healthy** *lifestyle.*

Another benefit is being able to focus on your future. An alcohol-free lifestyle allows you to care for your family and friends. Better relationships are a benefit of choosing not to use alcohol.

Staying alcohol free keeps you focused to achieve your life goals. *What are some activities you can do to help focus on your goals?*

Healthy Alternatives

When someone offers you alcohol, use your refusal skills as a healthful alternative. Refer to the S.T.O.P. strategy on the previous page. If you are offered alcohol, say no and explain why you have chosen not to drink. Offer a suggestion of an alcohol-free activity. If those steps do not work, promptly leave the area.

Finding another way to think or act will also help you avoid alcohol use. Instead of using alcohol, find a healthful way to spend your time. Join a club or sports group at school. Volunteer at a local organization, such as a food bank or animal shelter. Volunteering can give you a sense of purpose and can make you feel good about yourself. Another idea is to start a hobby or business with your friends. Alcohol use will never help you reach your goals, but positive activities such as these can help.

>>> **Reading Check**

DESCRIBE *What are benefits of choosing an alcohol-free lifestyle?* ■

>>> **After You Read**

1. **EXPLAIN** Describe how a person can get help for an alcohol problem.
2. **VOCABULARY** Define intervention. Use the term in a complete sentence.
3. **IDENTIFY** What is the best way to avoid problems with alcohol?

>>> **Thinking Critically**

4. **HYPOTHESIZE** How might you be affected if one of your close friends or family members developed an alcohol problem? Where could you find help? Explain your answer.
5. **ANALYZE** How can healthy alternatives prevent alcohol use?

>>> **Applying Health Skills**

6. **GOAL SETTING** Think about personal goals you have, such as going to college or the kind of job you would like to have some day. Write one or two of these on a sheet of paper. Leave space under each one. Use that space to explain how alcohol use could prevent you from reaching your goals.

⟳ Review

🔊 Audio

©BananaStock/PunchStock

Hands-On HEALTH ACTIVITY

Refusing *to Get into a* Car *with a Driver Who Has* Been Drinking

WHAT YOU WILL NEED

* 1 index card per student
* Colored pencils or markers

WHAT YOU WILL DO

1 Working with a small group, brainstorm a list of refusal statements a teen can use to avoid riding in a car with a driver who has been drinking.

2 Write a skit that has dialogue showing successful use of refusal skills. Be sure that every group member has a part.

3 Act out your skit for the class.

WRAPPING IT UP

As a class, discuss the dialogue used in each of the skits. Decide which skit presented the most effective refusal statements. Then, on your own, take your index card and write "Don't Ride with a Drunk Driver" on the card. Then, write at least two statements you can use to refuse such a ride. Use markers or colored pencils to make the card creative and colorful. Display your cards in the classroom.

You have learned that you should not drink and drive. You should also avoid getting into a car with someone who has been drinking. If someone who has been drinking alcohol invites you to ride in a car with him or her, you should know how to refuse that invitation. The following are some suggestions that can help you avoid an unsafe situation.

* Make a decision to never ride with someone who has been drinking, and stick to it.
* Do not make arrangements to go places with a driver who you know will likely drink at an event you are going to.
* Find other ways to get a ride home if you are with a driver who has been drinking.
* Use direct statements: "I am not riding with you. You have been drinking. Don't drive. I'll find us another ride."

Brand X Pictures

READING REVIEW

FOLDABLES and Other Study Aids

Take out the Foldable® that you created for Lesson 1 and any study organizers that you created for Lessons 2–4. Find a partner and quiz each other using these study aids.

LESSON 1 Alcohol Use and Teens

BIG IDEA Most teens do not use alcohol, but several factors influence teens to try it.

* Alcohol is a drug created by a chemical reaction in some foods, especially fruits and grains.
* Alcohol acts as a depressant by slowing down the functions and reactions of both the mind and body.
* Studies show that most teens do not use alcohol, but they do face a number of influences that encourage them to try it.
* Influences on teen alcohol use include peer pressure and images in the media.
* The negative effects of alcohol use pose even greater risks for teens than for adults.

LESSON 2 Effects of Alcohol Use

BIG IDEA Alcohol use has far-reaching effects to the body, other people, and personal relationships.

* Alcohol use has many short-term and long-term effects on a person's body.
* The use of alcohol has an immediate effect on many organs in a person's body, including the brain, stomach, heart, liver, and kidneys.
* A major factor in how a person reacts to alcohol use is blood alcohol concentration (BAC), or the amount of alcohol in the user's blood.
* Alcohol use affects all areas of a person's life.
* The use of alcohol can have negative effects on a person's thoughts and behavior.

LESSON 3 Alcoholism and Alcohol Abuse

BIG IDEA Alcohol is a highly addictive drug that can lead to disease and damage relationships.

* One of the greatest dangers of alcohol use is that it is habit-forming and can lead to addiction.
* Alcohol abuse is a serious health issue—an estimated 17 million people in the U.S. are either addicted to alcohol or have an alcohol problem.
* The disease of alcoholism results from a spiral of addiction and has physical, mental/emotional, and social consequences.
* Alcoholism is different from alcohol abuse, in which a person is not physically dependent on alcohol, but alcohol abuse is still a form of substance abuse.
* Alcoholism also affects families, friends, and society.

LESSON 4 Getting Help for Alcohol Abuse

BIG IDEA Many resources are available to help alcoholics, alcohol abusers, and their families.

* Family, friends, and various organizations can all help someone who has an alcohol problem.
* An intervention is a gathering where family and friends attempt to get a problem drinker to agree to seek help.
* Support groups can help alcoholics recover from their addiction and help families and friends of alcoholics learn to deal with the problem.
* Choosing not to use alcohol is the best way to avoid the dangers it poses to all aspects of a person's health.

 Review

 Web Quest

ASSESSMENT

Reviewing Vocabulary *and* Main Ideas

› inhibitions
› alcohol

› blood alcohol
concentration (BAC)

› cirrhosis
› binge drinking

› intoxicated

» On a sheet of paper, write the numbers 1–6. After each number, write the term from the list that best completes each statement.

LESSON 1 Alcohol Use and Teens

1. The type of _____ found in beverages such as beer, wine, and liquor is one of the most widely used and abused drugs in the U.S.

2. Consuming a lot of alcohol very quickly, or _____, is very dangerous and can cause death.

3. Drinking can cause people to lose their _____, or act in ways that are not typical for that person.

LESSON 2 Effects of Alcohol Use

4. A person becomes _____ if he or she drinks more alcohol than his or her body can tolerate.

5. A person's size and gender, along with how much he or she drinks and how fast, can affect that person's _____.

6. Heavy drinkers are at risk of developing _____, a potentially deadly condition in which normal liver cells turn into scar tissue.

» On a sheet of paper, write the numbers 7–12. Write *True* or *False* for each statement below. If the statement is false, change the underlined word or phrase to make it true.

LESSON 3 Alcoholism and Alcohol Abuse

7. Using alcohol regularly can lead to <u>addiction</u>.

8. The cycle of addiction to alcohol includes abuse, <u>malnutrition</u>, and addiction.

9. Alcohol abuse is a type of <u>substance abuse</u>.

LESSON 4 Getting Help for Alcohol Abuse

10. During an <u>enabler</u>, family and friends can discuss their concerns and try to convince an abuser to stop using alcohol.

11. An alcoholic may go through <u>resolution</u> when he or she suddenly stops using alcohol.

12. A <u>recovering alcoholic</u> is someone who has an addiction to alcohol but chooses to live without it.

 eAssessment

>> Using complete sentences, answer the following questions on a sheet of paper.

Thinking Critically

13. EVALUATE How can alcohol use as a teen cause health problems later in life?

14. ANALYZE Why is an alcoholic always said to be recovering rather than cured?

15. APPLY Imagine you are planning a birthday party for a friend. What are some fun activities you could choose that do not include the use of alcohol?

16. EVALUATE Explain how avoiding alcohol can have a positive effect. Be certain to include physical, mental/emotional, and social effects.

Write About It

17. EXPOSITORY WRITING Write a short advertisement encouraging teens to be alcohol free. Be sure to include ways to say no to negative peer influences and stay alcohol free.

18. OPINION What reasons might teens use to persuade others to use alcohol? What are some refusal responses to these statements?

STANDARDIZED TEST PRACTICE

Reading

Anish made the following concept map to organize his ideas for a paper. Review his concept map and then answer questions 1–3.

1. Under which subtopic should details about how alcohol affects the brain be placed?
   A. Drunk driving
   B. Affects relationships
   C. Harm body and mind
   D. Affects decision making

2. Which detail below supports the subtopic "Underage drinking illegal"?
   A. Binge drinking may lead to death.
   B. Alcohol is found in three forms: beer, liquor, and wine.
   C. It is illegal for anyone under the age of 21 to use alcohol.
   D. Alcoholism can be treated.

3. Based on this writing plan, what type of paper is Anish planning to write?
   A. a persuasive essay to convince teens not to drink alcohol
   B. a narrative that describes a personal experience with alcohol
   C. an explanatory paper that discusses the physical effects of alcohol
   D. none of the above

HOW SUBSTANCES AFFECT THE BODY

Respiratory System

The organs that supply your blood with oxygen

CANCER | SLOWS THE RESPIRATORY SYSTEM

Nearly **450,000 people** in the U.S. **die** each year from **smoking** or exposure to **secondhand smoke.**

Digestive System

The organs that break down foods into substances your cells can use

DEHYDRATION | LIVER DISEASE | NAUSEA

STOMACH ULCERS | HEARTBURN | INTOXICATION

Skeletal + Muscular Systems

Your body is supported by your skeleton. Your muscles move your body and control your organs.

POOR BALANCE | OSTEOPOROSIS

Nervous System

Your body's message and control center

MEMORY LOSS | STROKE | DIZZINESS | SLOWS BRAIN AND NERVOUS SYSTEM FUNCTIONS

SEIZURES | DESTROYS BRAIN CELLS | ADDICTION

BLURRED VISION | VISION AND HEARING PROBLEMS | IRRITABILITY

SLEEPLESSNESS

Circulatory System

This system carries oxygen and nutrients to the cells, and waste products away from the cells.

HIGH BLOOD PRESSURE | SLOWS HEART RATE | HEART FAILURE

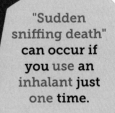

"Sudden sniffing death" **can occur if you use an inhalant just one time.**

 **TOBACCO**
 **ALCOHOL**
 **DRUGS**

WHAT'S IN TOBACCO?

If you use tobacco, here's what ends up inside you.

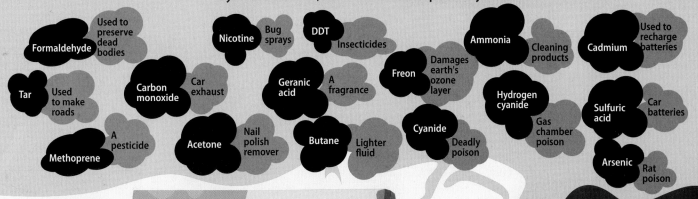

Formaldehyde	Used to preserve dead bodies
Tar	Used to make roads
Carbon monoxide	Car exhaust
Methoprene	A pesticide
Acetone	Nail polish remover
Nicotine	
Bug sprays	
Geranic acid	A fragrance
Butane	Lighter fluid
DDT	Insecticides
Freon	Damages earth's ozone layer
Cyanide	Deadly poison
Ammonia	Cleaning products
Hydrogen cyanide	Gas chamber poison
Cadmium	Used to recharge batteries
Sulfuric acid	Car batteries
Arsenic	Rat poison

55% of *high school* students have *never,* **EVER**, tried *cigarette smoking.*

Medicine misuse sends 700,000 people to the hospital in the United States each year.

ALCOHOL

Alcohol use affects EVERY aspect of your life, including your relationships, your school work, and your social activities.

Alcohol affects EVERY organ of your body.

SUPPORT GROUPS offer a place to:

 Share experiences with one another.

 Discuss difficulties.

 Learn effective ways to cope with problems.

 Encourage one another.

Alcohol **is a factor in nearly one-third of all traffic deaths in the United States.**

MEDICINES

Drugs that PROTECT your health can HARM your health if taken incorrectly.

DRUG MISUSE:

Misusing a drug means that you:

 Avoid following label instructions.

 Use a drug not prescribed for you.

 Use for longer than advised.

 Take more than the prescribed dose.

 Let someone else use a drug prescribed for you.

TEENS + ILLEGAL DRUGS

 NARCOTICS
Less than 3% have ever injected an illegal drug into their body.

 MARIJUANA
Less than 10% have tried marijuana.

 STIMULANTS
Less than 4% have ever tried methamphetamines.

Drug users are at higher risk for: HIV, all other STDs, hepatitis + tuberculosis.

Drugs

LESSONS

 **PREMIUM ONLINE RESOURCES**

 Audio

 Videos

 Bilingual Glossary

Fitness Zone

 Web Quest

Review

Drug Use *and* Abuse

BIG IDEA Using drugs affects your body, mind, emotions, and social life and can lead to consequences with the law.

Before You Read

QUICK WRITE List two legal drugs or types of medicine. Then list two drugs you know are illegal or harmful.

▶ **Video**

As You Read

FOLDABLES **Study Organizer**

Make the Foldable® on page 88 to record the information presented in Lesson 1.

Vocabulary

› drug
› drug misuse
› drug abuse

🔊 **Audio**

🔤 **Bilingual Glossary**

Developing Good Character

Citizenship Part of being a good citizen is helping to protect the health of others. The Partnership at Drugfree.org or the National Institute on Drug Abuse (NIDA) advocate for the health of others. *Conduct research on organizations like these to find out how you can get involved. Present your findings to the class. Encourage your peers to get involved too.*

WHAT IS A DRUG?

MAIN IDEA Some drugs can help heal the body, but drugs can also be harmful to your health.

You have likely heard the word *drug* many times before. A drug is *a substance other than food that changes the structure or function of the body or mind.* Some drugs are medicines, which may be able to save your life or the life of someone you love. Other drugs are illegal and dangerous.

All medicines are drugs, but not all drugs are medicines. Medicines prevent or cure illnesses or treat their symptoms. Some are available as over-the-counter (OTC) medicines, meaning you can find them on the shelf at a grocery store or pharmacy. Some OTC medicines can only be purchased by an adult, but most of them are available to anyone. Other medicines can only be legally obtained with a prescription, or written permission from a doctor.

> All *medicines* are **drugs,** but not all *drugs* are **medicines.**

All types of drugs, including medicines, can be misused or abused. It is important to be careful when using any drug, including medicine prescribed by your doctor. Whether you use an OTC medicine or a prescription drug, always closely read and follow the directions on the label. With a prescription medicine, your doctor will include instructions for how much to take, when to take it, and for how long. Some drugs are illegal because they are harmful to your health. However, even medicines that are legal can be dangerous if they are not used correctly. Medicines are only effective when they are used properly.

Reading Check

IDENTIFY *What are two categories of legal drugs?*

DRUG MISUSE AND ABUSE

MAIN IDEA Any drug can be harmful to your health if abused or misused.

As you have learned, illegal drugs as well as drugs that are medicines can be harmful if they are not used correctly. Many drugs are illegal for a good reason: they can be extremely dangerous or addictive. However, **drug misuse**, *taking or using medicine in a way that is not intended,* is also dangerous and can even lead to abusing drugs. A person who does any of the following is misusing drugs:

- Using the drug without following instructions on the label
- Using a drug not prescribed for you
- Allowing someone else to use a drug prescribed for you
- Taking more of the drug than the doctor prescribed
- Using the drug longer than advised by your doctor
Drug abuse is another danger to your health. **Drug abuse** is *intentionally using drugs in a way that is unhealthful or illegal.* When someone uses an illegal drug, such as marijuana or heroin, he or she is abusing drugs.

When someone uses legal drugs for nonmedical purposes, that person is also abusing drugs. Even prescription medicines can be dangerous if used improperly. You put your health at risk if you take prescription medicine that was not prescribed for you.

Misusing or abusing any drug can damage your body and lead to allergic reactions, illness, or even death. Drug abuse interferes with brain function, affecting your mental/emotional health. Some drugs make it difficult to concentrate, or they may cause depression or anxiety. Your social health is also affected. Teens who abuse drugs may withdraw from family and friends and lose interest in school or other activities.

> *Misusing* or **abusing** a drug **can damage** your body and lead to *allergic reactions,* **illness,** or even *death.*

Digital Vision/Getty Images

Knowing the facts about illegal drugs can help you avoid using drugs. *List resources for valid information about illegal drugs?*

Physical Consequences

Physical effects of drug use include sleeplessness, memory loss, irritability, nausea, heart failure, seizures, or stroke. If a drug user drives while taking drugs, that person is putting others at risk too. Many drug users develop an addiction. The symptoms of addiction can include:

TOLERANCE develops when a person uses a drug regularly. The user needs more and more of the drug to get the same effect.

CRAVING is a primary symptom of addiction. A person will feel a strong need, desire, or urge to use drugs and will feel anxious if he or she cannot use them.

LOSS OF CONTROL causes a person to take more drugs than he or she meant to take. Drug use may also happen at an unplanned time or place.

PHYSICAL DEPENDENCE makes it very difficult to quit using a drug. A person's body develops an actual physical need for drugs in order to function.

Drug use can reduce your motor skills, or the ability to move your muscles in normal ways. Simple tasks such as writing, speaking, or walking can be affected. This type of damage can often be permanent. Drug use can also have negative effects on teen growth and development.

Mental *and* Emotional Consequences

Drug abuse weakens a person's ability to think and learn, even though the person may not realize it at the time. Some drugs kill brain cells. The brain damage that results can interfere with the user's ability to think.

Using drugs keeps you from learning to handle difficult emotions in healthful ways. Drug users often experience depression, anxiety, and confusion. Drug use also often leads to poor decisions and bad judgment. It can cause a person to engage in other risk behaviors.

Social Consequences

Drug abuse can change someone's personality, cause mood swings, or even lead to violence. Drug users often have low self-esteem and difficulty dealing with others, even those closest to them. A person addicted to drugs will start to think only of his or her need for the drug.

Teens who abuse drugs can also lose their friends. Some may end their friendships or lie to friends in order to cover up their addictions. After a while, obtaining and using the drug becomes more important than maintaining relationships with friends.

Teens who use drugs often miss school or do not learn well because they cannot pay attention. Teens may not be able to participate in school activities if they are caught using drugs. As a result, they lose the opportunity to learn new skills or have interesting new experiences. Teens who abuse drugs often hurt their chances of reaching their long-term goals, such as going to college or having a career.

In females, drug use can negatively affect:

- height
- weight
- onset of first menstrual cycle
- regularity of periods
- breast development
- function of ovaries
- pregnancy
- the health of unborn babies

In males, drug use can negatively affect:

- height
- weight
- male hormone levels
- testicle size and function
- muscle mass and development
- the age at which the voice gets lower
- the age at which body and facial hair increases

The use of illegal drugs can have serious health consequences during the teen years. *Name two reasons why drug use is especially harmful to teens.*

>>> **Reading Check**

DESCRIBE *How can drug use affect a person's emotional health?*

DRUG USE AND THE LAW

MAIN IDEA Using drugs can lead to problems with the law.

The legal consequences of drug use are one of the many negative effects of this harmful behavior. Most drug use is illegal and dangerous. Federal and state laws say that harmful and addictive drugs may not be used or sold. When someone is caught using illegal drugs, the legal consequences are very serious. Teens may be arrested for possession of drugs. Teens can spend time in a detention center or be sentenced to probation where they must regularly check in with a court officer. Often they and their parents may have to pay fines. Teens can also get a criminal record.

A strong connection exists between drug use and crime. Someone who uses drugs may steal the drugs or steal money to buy the drugs. Stealing can lead to acts of violence, which increase the chances of being caught and sent to jail.

A **strong connection** exists between *drug use* and *crime*.

The legal consequences of drug use can also impact a teen's social health. A criminal record can last forever. Such a background can restrict access to certain jobs. A criminal record can also affect relationships with family and friends.

>>> **Reading Check**

EXPLAIN *How can drug abuse lead to crime?* ■

Selling or just having illegal drugs can result in serious legal consequences. *What is one legal consequence of using illegal drugs?*

REVIEW

>>> **After You Read**

1. **VOCABULARY** Define *drug misuse*. Give at least one example in a complete sentence.
2. **LIST** Name three physical effects drugs can have on a person's body.
3. **DESCRIBE** How could using illegal drugs negatively affect your social health?

>>> **Thinking Critically**

4. **EVALUATE** What is the difference between using drugs as medicine and abusing drugs?
5. **ANALYZE** Why is a person who uses drugs more likely to be involved in a crime?

>>> **Applying Health Skills**

6. **ACCESS INFORMATION** Use online or library resources to research drug misuse and abuse in the United States. Create a pamphlet or electronic presentation to educate others about the dangers.

 Review

🔊 Audio

Types *of* Drugs *and* Their Effects

BIG IDEA All types of illegal drugs have both short- and long-term effects.

Before You Read

QUICK WRITE List two illegal drugs you know about. Then briefly describe how these two drugs are harmful to a person's health.

 Video

As You Read

STUDY ORGANIZER Make the study organizer on page 88 to record the information presented in Lesson 2.

Vocabulary

› marijuana
› stimulant
› depressant
› hallucinogen
› narcotics
› club drugs
› inhalant
› anabolic steroids

 Audio

ABC Bilingual Glossary

MARIJUANA

MAIN IDEA Marijuana is a drug that alters brain processes.

Marijuana comes from *dried leaves and flowers of the hemp plant, called cannabis sativa.* It is an illegal drug that is usually smoked. You may have heard the different terms that people use when referring to marijuana, such as *pot* or *weed*.

Marijuana has a strong effect on the brain of a person who uses the drug. A chemical in marijuana changes the way the brain processes what a person sees, feels, hears, and perceives. Marijuana use can cause a variety of reactions in people. Some users may feel a pleasant sensation, but others do not react well to this drug. It is important to know that marijuana use harms the body in many ways. It has both short-term and long-term effects on body systems.

Short-Term Effects

Marijuana use increases reaction time and reduces coordination. It also increases heart rate and appetite. High doses of marijuana can cause anxiety and panic attacks.

Marijuana use *harms* the body in many *ways.*

Long-Term Effects

Marijuana users risk developing lung disease or cancer. The drug has many of the same harmful chemicals as tobacco smoke. In fact, the marijuana plant contains more than 400 chemicals. As with many drugs, marijuana use over time can cause depression, personality changes, or trouble at school or work. It can also affect relationships with friends and family.

Reading Check

EXPLAIN *How does marijuana affect the user?*

What Teens Want to Know

Teen Brain Development Studies by the National Institute of Mental Health show that the teen brain is very different from the brain of an adult. The part of the brain that helps you foresee control impulses and foresee consequences of your actions is not fully developed in teens. This is a factor that makes it especially dangerous for teens to try drugs.

Royalty-Free/Corbis

STIMULANTS, DEPRESSANTS, AND CLUB DRUGS

MAIN IDEA Stimulants, depressants, and club drugs have many negative effects on the body.

A stimulant (STIM·yuh·luhnt) is *a drug that speeds up the body's functions.* Stimulants raise the heart rate, blood pressure, and metabolism. A depressant (di•PRE•suhnt) is *a drug that slows down the body's functions and reactions, including heart and breathing rates.* Stimulants and depressants affect the body in opposite ways. Club drugs are *illegal drugs that are found mostly in nightclubs or at all-night dance parties called raves.* These are often used in social settings and are very dangerous.

Stimulants

Stimulants cause the heart to beat faster. Blood pressure and metabolism also rise. Someone who uses a stimulant will often move or speak more quickly than normal. That person may also feel excited or even anxious.

Illegal stimulants include cocaine, crack, and methamphetamine (meth). Some stimulants are legal and not necessarily harmful, such as caffeine found in coffee, tea, soda, and chocolate. Doctors sometimes prescribe stimulants to their patients for certain problems. However, stimulant abuse can be dangerous. See the figure below to view the harmful effects of different types of stimulants.

Depressants

In contrast to stimulants, depressants slow down a person's motor skills and coordination. They can affect someone mentally and emotionally by giving a false sense of well-being through feelings of reduced anxiety or relaxation. However, when a depressant wears off, the user may experience extreme mood swings or depression.

Most depressants come in tablet or capsule form. Depressants are legal when prescribed by a doctor to treat certain conditions. For example, doctors sometimes prescribe tranquilizers or barbiturates to treat people who suffer from anxiety or sleep disorders. Alcohol is also a depressant. It is illegal for people under the age of 21 to purchase alcohol. Misuse and abuse of depressants, including alcohol, can lead to coma or even death. The risk is even higher when a person combines alcohol with a depressant drug.

The biggest risk associated with stimulant abuse is damage to your heart, sometimes causing heart attacks or death. *What are some other harmful effects of stimulant abuse?*

Substance	Other Names	Forms	Methods of Use	Harmful Effects
Amphetamine	Crystal, ice, glass, crank, speed, uppers	Pills, powder, chunky crystals	Swallowed, snorted up the nose, smoked, injected	Uneven heartbeat, rise in blood pressure, physical collapse, stroke, heart attack, and death
Methamphetamine	Meth, crank, speed, ice	Pills, powder, crystals	Swallowed, snorted up the nose, smoked, injected	Memory loss, damage to heart and nervous system, seizures, and death
Cocaine	Coke, dust, snow, flake, blow, girl	White powder	Snorted up the nose, injected	Damage to nose lining and liver; heart attack, seizures, stroke, and death
Crack	Crack, freebase rocks, rock	Off-white rocks or chunks	Smoked, injected	Damage to lungs if smoked, seizures, heart attack, and death

Club Drugs

Club drugs are often used to make people feel more relaxed in a social setting. They are often made in home laboratories. Club drugs may be mixed with other drugs or harmful chemicals. **ECSTASY** increases the heart rate and body temperature, which can damage a person's organs. A person using Ecstasy may experience tingly skin or clenched jaws. He or she can also feel anxious and paranoid.

ROHYPNOL makes a person's blood pressure drop. The user feels dizzy and very sleepy. This drug also causes blackouts and memory loss. Rohypnol typically comes in pill form, although it can be crushed into a powder. It is also a drug that the user may not know that he or she has been given. If added to a drink, for example, it can make a person unconscious. As a result, this drug is unfortunately used to commit the crime of date rape.

KETAMINE, an anesthetic used in medical procedures, can be deadly if abused. It causes hallucinations, and people who use it often experience memory loss. An overdose of ketamine can cause a person to stop breathing.

>>> **Reading Check**
COMPARE AND CONTRAST *What is the main difference between the way stimulants and depressants affect the body?*

HALLUCINOGENS

MAIN IDEA > Hallucinogens are dangerous drugs that mainly affect the user's mind.

Hallucinogens (huh·LOO·suhn·uh·jenz) are *drugs that distort moods, thoughts, and senses.* These drugs interfere with thought processes and the ability to communicate. Hallucinogen users may become disoriented or confused. Strange behavior is common because the user can no longer tell what is real and what is not.

LSD (acid) and PCP (angel dust) are common hallucinogens. LSD is one of the strongest. It may come in tablet form or on absorbent paper. Someone who uses LSD may not know who or where they are. Harmful behaviors are common with LSD use. Users may even have terrifying flashbacks weeks or months after using the drug. The effects of PCP are similar to those of LSD.

>>> **Reading Check**
DETERMINE *Name three harmful effects of LSD.*

Hallucinogens can cause many harmful effects, including death. *What are two examples of hallucinogens?*

Substance	Other Names	Forms	Methods of Use	Harmful Effects
PCP	Angel dust, supergrass, killer weed, rocket fuel	White powder, liquid	Applied to leafy materials and smoked	Loss of coordination; increased heart rate, blood pressure, and body temperature; convulsions; heart and lung failure; broken blood vessels; bizarre or violent behavior; temporary psychosis; false feeling of having superpowers
LSD	Acid, blotter, microdot, white lightning	Tablets; squares soaked on paper	Eaten or licked	Increased blood pressure, heart rate, and body temperature; chills, nausea, tremors and sleeplessness; unpredictable behavior; flashbacks; false feeling of having superpowers

NARCOTICS

MAIN IDEA Not all narcotics are illegal, but all are extremely addictive.

Narcotics (nar·KAH·tics) are *drugs that get rid of pain and dull the senses.* These are highly addictive drugs. Historically, narcotics have been made from opium—a plant liquid that can numb the body. When used under a doctor's supervision, narcotics such as morphine and codeine are effective in treating extreme pain. However, laws control how all narcotics are sold and used because they are so addictive.

Heroin

Heroin is an illegal narcotic made from morphine. It is often inhaled or injected and sometimes smoked. Injecting the drug gives users a pleasant feeling. However, this feeling quickly wears off, and the user experiences symptoms of withdrawal.

These symptoms may include nausea, cramps, and vomiting. People who use heroin risk unconsciousness and death. Since it is usually injected, heroin users also risk HIV or hepatitis infection from shared needles. Because it is highly addictive, users commonly experience tolerance and dependence.

Oxycodone

Oxycodone is available legally through a doctor's prescription. When used as directed, it can control severe pain in patients with cancer and other diseases. However, oxycodone is also frequently abused. The long-term effect of using the drug is increased tolerance, which leads to physical addiction.

》》》 Reading Check

IDENTIFY *Name two types of narcotics that may be used as medicine when prescribed by a health care professional.*

Think of all the ways you can have fun without using drugs. *What are some drug-free activities that you and your friends enjoy?*

Health Effects of Narcotic Drug Abuse

Can cause drowsiness, constipation, and depressed breathing.

Taking a large single dose could cause severe respiratory depression or death.

Can cause death if taken with certain medications or alcohol.

Can lead to physical dependence and tolerance. The body becomes used to the substance and higher doses are needed to feel the same initial effect.

Narcotics are highly addictive, often causing uncontrollable drug use in spite of negative consequences.

Withdrawal symptoms occur if use is reduced abruptly. Symptoms can include restlessness, muscle and bone pain, insomnia, diarrhea, vomiting, cold flashes with goose bumps, and involuntary leg movements.

Withdrawal from narcotics usually requires detoxification in a hospital. Although withdrawal is often a painful experience, it is not life-threatening.

When narcotics are abused, there is a risk of addiction and other health consequences. *What are some of these consequences?*

SOMOS/SuperStock

INHALANTS

MAIN IDEA Using inhalants can cause brain damage and even death.

Inhalants (in·HAY·luhntz) are *the vapors of chemicals that are sniffed or inhaled to get a "high."* Most come from toxic household products. Toxic inhalants include hairspray, lighter fluid, air freshener, cleaning products, markers or pens, and paint. Inhalant use can cause nausea, dizziness, confusion, and loss of motor skills.

Inhalant use sends poisons straight to the brain. Inhalants cause permanent damage and affect a person's ability to walk, talk, or think. Inhalant abuse, even if it is only the first time, can also kill the user instantly. Experimenting with inhalants can cause death from choking, suffocation, or heart attack.

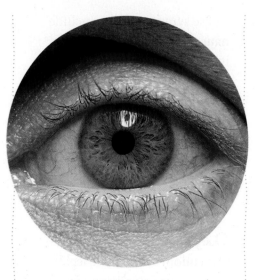

One symptom of inhalant abuse is red or runny eyes. *What other parts of the body can inhalant abuse damage?*

Warning Signs *of* Inhalant Abuse

A person who uses inhalants often shows symptoms of the abuse. Some common symptoms are listed below. If you notice these symptoms in someone you know, speak to a teacher or trusted adult about your concerns.

- Eyes that are red or runny
- Sores or spots near the mouth
- Breath that smells strange or like chemicals
- Holding a marker or pen near the nose

>>> **Reading Check**

GIVE EXAMPLES *What are two symptoms of inhalant abuse?*

Health SKILLS ACTIVITY

Accessing Information

Marijuana *Myths*

Marijuana is the most commonly used illegal drug. Because its effects are not as dramatic as some other illegal drugs, it is often mistakenly believed to be a harmless drug. Here are some common myths about marijuana use:

Myth: "Marijuana is not addictive. Users can stop whenever they want."

Myth: "Smoking marijuana is safer than using other drugs."

Myth: "Everyone smokes marijuana."

On Your Own

Using this lesson and other reliable online or print resources, find information that shows how these myths may not be true. Develop a fact sheet listing each myth and the truths behind each myth.

STEROIDS

MAIN IDEA Steroid use can cause serious health problems.

Some drugs mimic the behavior of chemicals made by the body. For example, anabolic steroids (a·nuh·BAH·lik STAIR·oydz) are *substances that cause muscle tissue to develop at an abnormally high rate.* Doctors sometimes legally prescribe steroids to treat growth problems, lung diseases, and skin conditions.

Any **nonmedical** use of *steroids* is **illegal.**

Some athletes use steroids to try to increase their body weight, strength, or endurance. However, steroid use causes a variety of serious health issues.

Effects include uncontrolled anger, shrunken testicles, severe acne, high blood pressure, and infertility. Females can develop a deeper voice, excess facial hair, and a masculine-looking body. Steroid use can also cause damage to other body systems.

Any nonmedical use of steroids is illegal. Athletes who use steroids can be dismissed from a team or an event. Illegal steroid users may also face fines and jail time. Athletes who are caught using steroids are often suspended or banned from their sport. Many have had their reputations damaged as a result.

>>> **Reading Check**

RECALL *How are anabolic steroids similar to chemicals in your body?* ■

The best way to improve your athletic performance is to practice. *How could using drugs stand in the way of reaching your goals?*

REVIEW

>>> **After You Read**

1. **VOCABULARY** Define depressant. Use the term in a complete sentence.
2. **EXPLAIN** What is the biggest long-term risk for marijuana users?
3. **SUMMARIZE** Name three types of drugs that are legal only when prescribed by a doctor.

>>> **Thinking Critically**

4. **APPLY** Suppose a friend told you inhalants were safe because they are items found in your own house. How would you respond? Is this valid health information?
5. **ANALYZE** What are some of the high-risk behaviors that could result from using hallucinogens or club drugs?

>>> **Applying Health Skills**

6. **ADVOCACY** Write a script for a public service announcement for radio or television, explaining the short- and long-term effects of narcotics use.

🔄 Review

🔊 Audio

Staying Drug Free

BIG IDEA Many reasons and resources exist to help teens and their families stay drug free.

Developing Good Character

Citizenship You can demonstrate good citizenship by encouraging others to stay drug free. Find out about programs in your school or community that educate teens on the dangers of drug use and tell your classmates about them. Identify what methods they use to reach teens and find out how students can get involved. *What programs would you be interested in participating in? Why?*

WHY DO SOME TEENS USE DRUGS?

MAIN IDEA Responding to peer pressure, the media, and personal problems can influence teens to try drugs.

Teens use drugs for many different reasons. For example, the media often show people enjoying alcohol or even drugs, particularly in TV shows or movies. These images can make some teens feel they will be like the happy, attractive people they see if they begin to drink alcohol or use drugs too.

What these images may not show are the problems addiction can cause. Often it appears that using drugs or alcohol is harmless or without consequence. However, drug and alcohol use can have serious effects on all sides of your health triangle. The media does sometimes offer helpful information about drugs and alcohol. Television reports and magazine articles can provide accurate health information about the effects of drugs on the brain and body, for example.

> **Drug** and **alcohol** use can have *serious* effects on all sides of your **health triangle.**

Additionally, teens might see adults in their lives using alcohol. Friends might pressure a teen to try drugs or alcohol. Peer pressure can have a strong influence even if it is negative. It can be difficult to say no to friends whose approval you would like.

Finally, some teens may try drugs to cope with emotional problems. To escape or forget, they may turn to <u>substance abuse,</u> or *using illegal or harmful drugs, including any use of alcohol while under the legal drinking age.* Substance abuse includes drug misuse and drug abuse.

>>> **Reading Check**

EXPLAIN *Describe the influence that peers can have on a teen's decision to use alcohol or drugs.*

Sue Smith/age fotostock

WAYS TO STAY DRUG FREE

MAIN IDEA Staying drug free has many benefits.

The choice to avoid illegal drugs and the improper use of legal drugs may be the most healthful decision you can make. Being substance free shows self-control. It means you have taken charge of your life and your health. It is important to make decisions that promote both a healthy body and mind. Staying drug free can be difficult, but it has many benefits.

Reasons *to* Avoid Drugs

Making wise choices about drugs will have a positive effect on your physical, mental/emotional, and social health. When you avoid drugs, you will have a greater chance of reaching your goals.

> These are a few activities you can enjoy without using alcohol or other drugs. *Can you think of some other positive alternatives to substance abuse?*

By deciding not to use drugs, you can enjoy these benefits:

- **Physical health** You show that you care for yourself and your health. You will not suffer the physical consequences of drug abuse on the body.
- **Control over your actions** You are better able to stay in control and act more responsibly.
- **Obeying the law** You show respect for the law and are a good citizen.
- **Protecting your future** You are able to set goals and work toward them. You are able to concentrate better and will do better in school.
- **Healthier relationships** You are able to enjoy other interests with family and friends.
- **Self-respect** You want to avoid harm to your body and mind. You can be confident about your decisions. You know you have made healthful choices.

The *choice* to **avoid illegal drugs** is the most *important* and *healthful* **decision** you could make.

Alternatives *to* Drug Use

If someone offers you drugs or alcohol, what would you do? You could suggest an alternative (ahl·TER·nuh·tihv), or *another way of thinking or acting.* Offering positive alternatives can help relieve some of the pressure you may be feeling. It also gives you the chance to be a positive influence on your peers. Possible alternatives include attending drug-free events and improving your talents and skills.

Fancy/Alamy

Have fun at drug-free and alcohol-free events. Avoid environments where alcohol and other drugs are present. Use positive peer pressure to help others avoid these environments.

Improve your talents or skills. Choose an activity you like, and practice it until you become an expert. Become a great skateboarder, a computer whiz, or the best artist at school.

Be part of a group. Join a sports team, a club, or a community group.

Start your own business. Make yourself available for babysitting, yard work, or other jobs. Let friends and neighbors know.

Refusing *Drugs*

Tyler has noticed that his best friend, Jonathan, has become a little distant. Jonathan recently changed schools, so Tyler no longer sees him every day. Tyler knows that Jonathan has made some new friends at his new school. When they get together, Tyler notices that Jonathan doesn't seem interested and has trouble following the conversation.

One day, Tyler meets up with Jonathan and some of his new friends. Jonathan's new friends suggest that everyone go back to Jonathan's house to smoke marijuana. Tyler wants to keep Jonathan as a friend, but he doesn't want to use drugs. What should Tyler do?

Apply the S.T.O.P. formula to Tyler's situation.
- **S**ay no in a firm voice.
- **T**ell why not.
- **O**ffer other ideas.
- **P**romptly leave.

Explain how Tyler might use this strategy to refuse the harmful suggestion made by Jonathan's friends.

Saying No *to* Drugs

Developing skills to refuse drugs is very important. The best way to avoid being pressured to use illegal substances is to use refusal skills. Refusal skills can help you say no to other unhealthy behaviors as well. You can resist negative peer pressure without feeling guilty or uncomfortable. Saying no in a clear and confident way lets others know you respect yourself and your health. If you feel pressure to experiment with drugs, remember the S.T.O.P. strategy: **S**ay no in a firm voice; **T**ell why not; **O**ffer alternative ideas or activities; and if all else fails, **P**romptly leave.

This strategy is helpful when you are faced with a difficult situation. However, you can also take steps to help you avoid even having to use your refusal skills.

You can choose to make friends with people who have also chosen to avoid drugs. Friends who are committed to being drug free will support your decision and help you avoid situations where drugs or alcohol may be present. You can also look for healthful ways to deal with whatever issues you may face. If you feel lonely or depressed, or if you need help solving a personal problem, talk to a parent or another adult you trust. Making wise choices about how you spend your time, who your friends are, and how you deal with your feelings can all have a positive effect on your ability to be drug free.

>>> **Reading Check**

IDENTIFY *What are two positive alternatives to drug use?*

Friends can be an important influence during the teen years. *How can friends help you stay drug free?*

©Purestock/PunchStock

HELP FOR DRUG USERS AND THEIR FAMILIES

MAIN IDEA Resources are available to help drug users and their families face substance abuse.

Stopping drug abuse after it has started is much harder than resisting drugs in the first place. Some effects of drug abuse are permanent. However, drug addiction is treatable. Many resources are available to help drug users overcome the pattern of addiction.

Drug Treatment Options

Drug addiction is a disease. Treatment requires changes in behavior. People who are addicted to drugs must first admit that they have a problem. Then they need to seek help to recover. In some cases, **drug rehabilitation** is needed. This is *a process in which a person relearns how to live without an abused drug.* Sometimes a drug abuser may enter a treatment facility.

Support groups allow people to work together to help stay drug free. Often, recovering addicts find strength from talking with other people who are working toward the same goal.

Regular meetings encourage these positive relationships. Support groups for addiction include Narcotics Anonymous and Cocaine Anonymous.

Some people find the support and help they need to stay drug free through counseling. Counseling provides an opportunity to openly share thoughts and feelings with a trained expert. It can help addicts deal with their psychological dependency on drugs. Counseling may involve only the addict or the person's entire family.

Help *for* Families

When someone is addicted to drugs, that person's family also needs help. One of the many resources for families is Nar-Anon. Like Al-Anon, Nar-Anon helps family members learn how to deal with the problems caused by drug addiction.

>>> **Reading Check**

RECALL *What are some drug treatment options?* ■

Support from friends can help you stay substance free. *What resources are available in your community for teens with substance abuse problems?*

Design Pics/Don Hammond

LESSON 3

REVIEW

>>> **After You Read**

1. **VOCABULARY** Define *drug rehabilitation.* Use it in a complete sentence.
2. **LIST** What are two reasons why some teens might choose to use drugs?
3. **DESCRIBE** What are some of the ways support groups help people become drug free?

>>> **Thinking Critically**

4. **EVALUATE** How can suggesting a positive alternative to alcohol or drug use help you stay substance free? Explain your answer.
5. **APPLY** What do you think is the most important reason for you to stay drug free? Explain your reasoning in a short paragraph.

>>> **Applying Health Skills**

6. **REFUSAL SKILLS** Think about ways to say no to harmful behaviors. Team up with a classmate. Role-play a situation where you use these strategies to say no to illegal drugs.

🔄 Review

🔊 Audio

Hands-On HEALTH ACTIVITY

Memory Obstacles

Many drugs make it difficult to process information. In this activity, loud music and disruptive talk mimics the effects of some drugs. How will these distractions interfere with your ability to recall information?

WHAT YOU WILL NEED

* Paper for each member of the group
* Pencil for each member of the group
* 2 posters with 25 pictures of everyday items on each
* A source of loud music

WHAT YOU WILL DO

1 Using pictures from magazines, one person in the group will make 2 posters with 25 everyday items on each one.

2 The leader will hold up the first poster and give the group 30 seconds to look at it. Each student should try to remember as many items as possible.

3 The leader then puts the poster down, and the students write down as many of the items as they can recall.

4 Now loud music is turned on. The leader also asks two people on opposite sides of the room to have a loud conversation with each other.

5 Then the leader holds up the second poster and repeats step 3.

WRAPPING IT UP

How many people in the group had more trouble remembering items on the second poster than on the first? Why? Compare what just happened in your group to what can happen to your brain when under the influence of a drug.

Getty Images/SW Productions

READING REVIEW

FOLDABLES and Other Study Aids

Take out the Foldable® that you created for Lesson 1 and any study organizers that you created for Lessons 2–3. Find a partner and quiz each other using these study aids.

LESSON 1 Drug Use and Abuse

BIG IDEA Using drugs affects your body, mind, emotions, and social life and can lead to consequences with the law.

* Drugs can be medicines that help the body, but many drugs are harmful to your health.
* Any drug can be harmful to your health if abused or misused.
* Drug misuse, or taking medicine in a way that is not intended, is dangerous and can lead to drug abuse.
* Drug abuse is intentionally using drugs in a way that is unhealthful or illegal.
* Using drugs can result in serious legal problems, including arrest, fines, jail time, and a criminal record.

LESSON 2 Types of Drugs and Their Effects

BIG IDEA All types of illegal drugs have both short- and long-term effects.

* Marijuana is an illegal drug that affects the body.
* Stimulants come in several forms and have effects on the user.
* Common stimulants include caffeine, which is legal, along with illegal drugs such as cocaine.
* Depressants slow down the body and mind and affect a person's motor skills and coordination.
* Many depressants are legal when prescribed by a doctor, but they are often misused or abused.

* Drugs that are considered to be hallucinogens, such as LSD, PCP, and Ecstasy, affect the user's mind and have dangerous effects.
* Club drugs are often used in social settings and can result in dangerous consequences.
* Not all narcotics are illegal, but these types of drugs are all extremely addictive.
* Using inhalants, even for the first time, can cause brain damage and even death.
* Anabolic steroid use can cause many serious health problems, including anger issues, shrunken testicles in males, masculine characteristics in females, severe acne, heart disease, certain types of cancer, and damage to other body systems.

LESSON 3 Staying Drug Free

BIG IDEA Many reasons and resources exist to help teens and their families stay drug free.

* Responding to peer pressure, the media, and personal problems can influence teens to try drugs.
* Practicing refusal skills can help you stay drug free.
* Staying drug free can benefit all sides of your health triangle—physical, mental/emotional, and social.
* Resources are available to help drug users and their families deal with the problems of substance abuse and break the pattern of addiction.

Review

Web Quest

ASSESSMENT

Reviewing Vocabulary *and* Main Ideas

> depressant
> drug

> hallucinogens
> drug misuse

> marijuana
> inhalants

> drug abuse
> stimulant

>> On a sheet of paper, write the numbers 1–8. After each number, write the term from the list that best completes each statement.

LESSON 1 **Drug Use and Abuse**

1. _____ involves taking or using medicine in a way that is not intended.

2. When someone takes an illegal drug, such as marijuana or heroin, that person is engaging in _____.

3. A _____ is a substance other than food that changes the structure or function of the body or mind.

LESSON 2 **Types of Drugs and Their Effects**

4. _____ are drugs that distort the moods, thoughts, and senses of the user.

5. _____ include any substance whose fumes are sniffed and inhaled to produce mind-altering sensations.

6. The most commonly used illegal drug is _____.

7. A drug that raises the heart rate, blood pressure, and metabolism is called a _____.

8. A _____ slows down a person's motor skills and coordination and can affect a user mentally and emotionally.

>> On a sheet of paper, write the numbers 9–14. Write *True* or *False* for each statement below. If the statement is false, change the underlined word or phrase to make it true.

LESSON 3 **Staying Drug Free**

9. Another way of thinking or acting is called an <u>alternative</u>.

10. The use of illegal or harmful drugs is called <u>rehabilitation</u>.

11. <u>Support groups</u> allow people to work together to help stay drug free.

12. <u>Few</u> resources are available to help drug users and their families deal with substance abuse.

13. The <u>S.T.O.P. strategy</u> involves saying no in a firm voice, telling why not, offering positive alternative ideas or activities, and promptly leaving if all else fails.

14. A process in which an addicted person learns how to live without drugs is called <u>refusal skills</u>.

✔ eAssessment

>> Using complete sentences, answer the following questions on a sheet of paper.

Thinking Critically

15. HYPOTHESIZE What are three reasons someone might begin experimenting with drugs?

16. HYPOTHESIZE Why might someone ignore the risks of drug use?

Write About It

17. NARRATIVE WRITING Write a story about a teen athlete who is considering using steroids.

18. EXPOSITORY WRITING Write a paragraph describing how a teen can use positive peer pressure to influence others to avoid using drugs.

STANDARDIZED TEST PRACTICE

Reading
Read the two paragraphs and then answer the questions.

Heroin is a highly addictive drug that relieves pain and dulls the senses. Heroin users usually inject the drug into their body. The drug gives users a sense of euphoria, or a feeling of intense joy. This feeling is short-lived, however. Soon after, the users suffer from withdrawal, which can be extremely painful.

Because the symptoms of heroin withdrawal are so painful, users must go through a detoxification process. Most need professional help to quit. The process may include doses of legal drugs that relieve the withdrawal symptoms. One of the drugs used in heroin detoxification is called methadone. It is a synthetic drug not found in nature. It delays the feelings and cravings that users experience during withdrawal.

1. In the first paragraph, euphoria means
   A. a feeling of pain.
   B. a feeling of fullness.
   C. a feeling of intense joy.
   D. None of the above

2. From the information in the second paragraph, the reader can conclude that heroin
   A. is a safe drug.
   B. can be used with moderation.
   C. can be given up easily by users.
   D. is a dangerous and addictive drug.

3. According to the second paragraph, many heroin users must go through a detoxification process in order to quit because
   A. withdrawal symptoms are so painful.
   B. it is required by the law.
   C. it stops cravings for other drugs, as well.
   D. None of the above

Using Medicines Wisely

LESSONS

PREMIUM ONLINE RESOURCES ❯  Audio Videos Bilingual Glossary

 Fitness Zone Web Quest Review

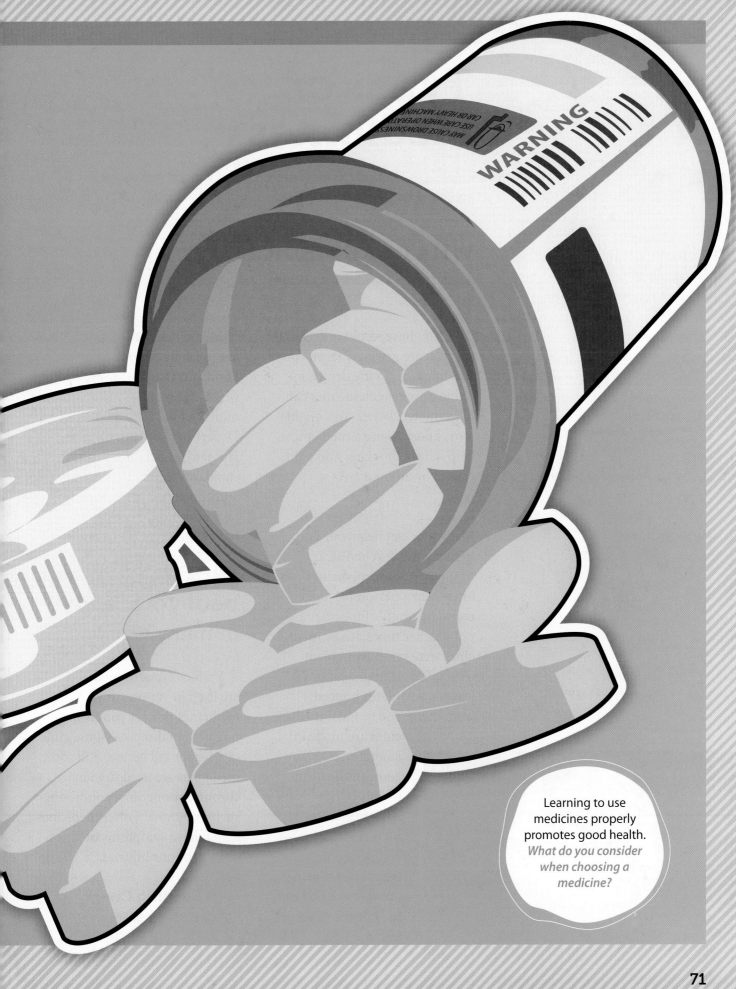

Learning to use medicines properly promotes good health. *What do you consider when choosing a medicine?*

Types *of* Medicines

BIG IDEA Using medicines wisely is a sign of good personal and consumer health.

>>> **Before You Read**

QUICK WRITE Describe a time when you used a medicine. State what the medicine was intended to treat and how you used it.

▶ Video

>>> **As You Read**

FOLDABLES Study Organizer

Make the Foldable® on page 89 to record the information presented in Lesson 1.

>>> **Vocabulary**

› medicine
› vaccine
› antibiotics
› over-the-counter (OTC) medicine
› prescription medicine

🔊 Audio

🔤 Bilingual Glossary

Myth vs. Fact

Myth: Only babies and toddlers need vaccines.

Fact: Several important vaccines are required for those between the ages of 10 and 18. Most preteens and teens will need to receive a vaccine or booster shot for diphtheria and tetanus, chicken pox, hepatitis B, measles, mumps, and rubella, and meningococcus.

WHAT ARE MEDICINES?

MAIN IDEA A medicine is a drug that can prevent or cure an illness or ease its symptoms.

If you have a cold or feel as if you are getting a fever, you might go to the drugstore to buy some medicine that can help you feel better. You might also choose to use a medicine to help relieve the aches and pains caused by an injury. A medicine is *a drug that prevents or cures an illness or eases its symptoms.* Medicines can help your body in many ways. When sickness or injury occurs, medicines can often help a person feel better or recover from the illness.

In earlier times, many medicines were taken from plant leaves. People might eat the leaves or drink tea brewed from them. Today, most medicines are made in laboratories. Many come in the form of pills or liquids and are swallowed. Medicines may also be injected into the bloodstream using needles, inhaled into the lungs, or rubbed into the skin.

Medicines in the United States are carefully controlled by the Food and Drug Administration (FDA). This agency is part of the federal government's Department of Health and Human Services. The FDA sets standards for medicine safety and effectiveness. The agency tests and approves medicines before they can be sold.

Medicines can **help your body** in many ways.

Various types of medicines are used in various ways. Some medicines protect you from getting certain diseases. Some cure diseases or kill germs. Still some medicines are used to manage chronic, or ongoing, conditions such as asthma. Other medicines help relieve symptoms of illness or treat minor injuries.

>>> **Reading Check**

DEFINE *What are medicines?*

George Doyle/Getty Images

THE PURPOSE OF MEDICINES

MAIN IDEA Different medicines serve different purposes in the body.

Have you ever had to get a shot during a visit to a doctor or nurse? Sometimes, a doctor may give you a shot to help fight an illness. On other occasions, you may get a shot to help prevent a disease. A vaccine is one example of a type of medicine that is used to keep you from getting a disease. A medical professional may also give people certain medicines to help them recover from a disease or ease the symptoms of an illness. Scientists who focus on finding cures have developed medicines that help a sick person's body fight disease or infection. Others types of medicines can be used to relieve pain, soreness, or swelling.

Have you ever had to get a shot during a visit to a doctor or nurse?

Vaccines are medicines that prevent disease. *What are some vaccines that you may have received?*

Type of Medicine	Some Examples	Disease or Problem
Vaccines	• MMR vaccine • Varicella vaccine • HPV vaccine • Pertussis vaccine	• Measles, mumps, and rubella • Chicken pox • Human Papillomavirus • Whooping Cough
Antibiotics	• Penicillin • Cephalosporin • Tetracycline • Macrolides	• Strep throat, pneumonia, STDs • Meningitis, skin rash • Urinary tract infections, Rocky Mountain spotted fever • Given to patients allergic to penicillin
Pain Relievers	• Aspirin, acetaminophen, ibuprofen, codeine	• General pain relief

Various types of medicines are used to treat or prevent various illnesses. *What types of illnesses are antibiotics used to treat?*

Preventing Disease

A **vaccine** (vak·SEEN) is *a preparation of dead or weakened pathogens that is introduced into the body to cause an immune response.* Vaccines protect against diseases that can spread from person to person. When you are vaccinated, your body can make substances called antibodies that will attack or kill off the germs that cause a disease. Some vaccines provide protection for many years. Others, such as the flu vaccine, protect you for only about a year.

Fighting Germs

Antibiotics (an·tih·by·AH·tiks) are *medicines that reduce or kill harmful bacteria in the body.* An antibiotic may be prescribed to treat an infection. However, improper use can make bacteria resistant. That means certain antibiotics may no longer stop an infection. An antibiotic cannot help the body fight an illness such as the common cold. Other drugs are used to fight viruses and fungi.

Taking Medicine

Katie runs track. Because of all the training she does, Katie often has sore muscles. She takes an over-the-counter pain reliever for her sore muscles, but lately it hasn't been helping. What should Katie do?

Remember the six steps of the decision-making process:

1. State the situation.
2. List the options.
3. Weigh the possible outcomes.
4. Consider your values.
5. Make a decision and act on it.
6. Evaluate the decision.

Use these steps to determine what you would do if you were in Katie's situation.

Relieving Pain

Have you ever had sore muscles, a toothache, or a headache? If you took medicine to feel better, it was most likely a pain reliever. Pain relievers block pain signals sent through the nervous system. Many pain relievers are available as <u>over-the-counter (OTC) medicine,</u> or *a medicine that you can buy without a doctor's permission.* These include aspirin, ibuprofen, and acetaminophen. Aspirin can also reduce swelling. Some painkillers, such as codeine, treat more serious pain and are available only with a prescription. A <u>prescription</u> (prih·SKRIP·shuhn) <u>medicine</u> is *a medicine that can be obtained legally only with a doctor's written permission.* Prescription medicines require a written order because they typically carry more risks.

> Different medicines do different jobs. *Why are medicines regulated by the government?*

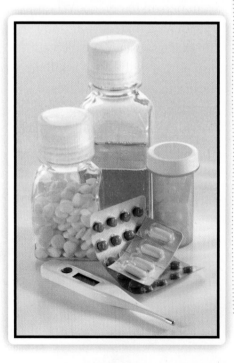

Managing Disease

Some medicines help people manage chronic diseases or conditions, such as allergies, asthma, diabetes, or mental illnesses such as anxiety and depression. People with diabetes take insulin to help control their blood sugar. People with allergies can take antihistamines to treat swelling and other allergy symptoms.

Often, medicine is taken by swallowing. However, medicine can be given in a number of different ways. The various methods of delivering medicine to the body include:

- **Swallowing, or ingestion.** A pill, tablet, capsule, or liquid moves through the stomach into the bloodstream and then through the body. Most pain relievers are taken this way.
- **Injection, or shot.** Injected medicines begin to work more quickly because they directly enter the bloodstream. These are administered by a needle that pierces the skin.
- **Inhalation.** Medicine can be inhaled, or breathed in, as a mist or fine powder. People with asthma may use an inhaler. Cold or sinus medication can also be inhaled through the nose.
- **Topical application.** Creams and ointments can be rubbed directly onto the skin. Patches containing medicine may also be applied to the skin.

⟫⟫ Reading Check

EXPLAIN *Name three different kinds of medicine, and tell what each does.*

PRESCRIPTION AND NON-PRESCRIPTION MEDICINES

MAIN IDEA Some medicines require a doctor's permission, while others are available without a prescription.

As you have learned, prescription medicine can be obtained only with a written order from a doctor. Written permission is required because prescription medicines carry more risks. You do not need a doctor's permission to buy an over-the-counter medicine. However, both prescription and over-the-counter medicines must be used very carefully.

If you are prescribed medicine, your doctor will write out instructions that explain how much to take, when to take it, and for how long. Prescriptions must be filled by a pharmacist who is trained to prepare and distribute medicines. Your doctor's instructions will appear on the prescription medicine label.

The FDA requires medicine labels to have specific information. Always read the label closely before taking any medicine, and follow the directions.

You can find over-the-counter (OTC) medicines in groceries and drugstores. They are considered safe to use without a doctor's permission. However, always be careful when you use OTC medicines. Follow the directions, because even OTC medicines can be harmful if not used correctly. If you have any questions about a medicine, ask a doctor or pharmacist.

>>> **Reading Check**

CONTRAST *What is the main difference between prescription and over-the-counter (OTC) medicines?* ◼

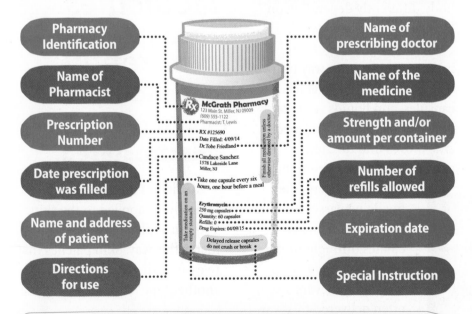

Pharmacy Identification

Name of Pharmacist

Prescription Number

Date prescription was filled

Name and address of patient

Directions for use

Name of prescribing doctor

Name of the medicine

Strength and/or amount per container

Number of refills allowed

Expiration date

Special Instruction

McGrath Pharmacy
123 Main St. Miller, NJ 09009
(609) 555-1122
Pharmacist: T. Lewis

• RX #125690
• Date Filled: 4/09/14
  Dr. Tobe Friedland

• Candace Sanchez
  1578 Lakeside Lane
  Miller, NJ

Take one capsule every six hours, one hour before a meal

Erythromycin
250 mg capsules
Quantity: 60 capsules
Refills: 0
Drug Expires: 04/09/15

Delayed release capsules — do not crush or break

Take medication on an empty stomach.

Finish all medication unless otherwise directed by a doctor.

Your doctor or pharmacist can help you understand a prescription medicine label. *What types of information can you find on a prescription medicine label?*

>>> **After You Read**

1. **VOCABULARY** Define the term *antibiotics*. Use it in an original sentence.

2. **NAME** What is the type of medicine that prevents a disease from developing?

3. **LIST** What are the four main purposes of medicines?

>>> **Thinking Critically**

4. **ANALYZE** A friend of yours on the football team wants an energy burst before a game. He wants to take a handful of vitamins. When you express concern, he says, "They're over-the-counter vitamins." Respond to this comment.

>>> **Applying Health Skills**

5. **APPLY** Lanie's doctor gave her a six-day prescription of an antibiotic for her sore throat. After only three days, all of her symptoms are gone. Should Lanie continue taking the antibiotic? Explain why or why not.

🔄 Review

🔊 Audio

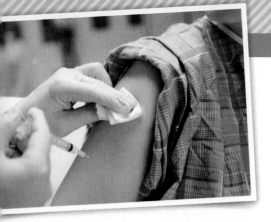

How Medicines Affect Your Body

BIG IDEA Medicines can contribute to good health when used properly.

Before You Read

QUICK WRITE Write about a time when you had to take medicine and how it affected you.

▶ Video

As You Read

STUDY ORGANIZER Make the study organizer on page 89 to record the information presented in Lesson 2.

Vocabulary

› side effect
› tolerance

🔊 Audio

Ⓐ Bilingual Glossary

HOW MEDICINES ENTER THE BODY

MAIN IDEA A medicine may be swallowed, injected, inhaled, or applied to the skin.

Different medicines are used in different ways. For example, a mild sunburn or an itchy mosquito bite could be treated with a cream or lotion. Another form of over-the-counter medicine could help relieve pain from a headache or a pulled muscle. A person with a serious illness may need prescription pills or injections. Medicines affect your body differently depending on how they are administered.

Swallowing, or ingestion, is the most common way to take medicines. Pills, tablets, capsules, and liquids are taken orally, or by mouth. The medicine moves into the stomach and small intestine. From the digestive system, the medicine passes into the bloodstream and circulates throughout the body. Cold medicines and pain relievers are often delivered this way.

Injection, or a shot, is another way that medicines can enter the body.

A needle injects the medicine directly into the bloodstream. Injected medicines begin to work more quickly than other types.

Inhalation is yet another delivery system. Medicine can be inhaled as a mist or fine powder. People with asthma often use inhalers. You can breathe in, or inhale, cold or sinus medication through your nostrils.

Medicines affect your body differently depending on how they are administered.

Medicines are also given topically, or applied to the skin. You can apply creams and ointments this way. Skin patches that release medicine over time are another type of topical medicine.

Reading Check

IDENTIFY *What is the most common way medicines are taken?*

🏃 Fitness Zone

When I get regular exercise and eat healthfully, I don't get sick very often. As a result, I don't need to take medicine very often and risk possible bad side effects. Physical activity helps me stay healthy. *How can a physical fitness routine contribute to your good health?*

PROBLEMS WITH MEDICINES

MAIN IDEA › Medicines affect different people in different ways.

Because every person's body is unique, medicines affect people in different ways. Combining medicines may also affect the way they work. Some medicines do not interact well with others and can cause harmful reactions. Some people are allergic to certain medicines and cannot take them at all. Your age, weight, and overall health can determine how a medicine affects you.

Side Effects

Medicines can help you, but if you do not use them properly, they can also hurt you. A side effect is *a reaction to a medicine other than the one intended.* Sometimes, side effects are simply unpleasant. For example, a medicine might make you feel sick to your stomach, sleepy, dizzy, or cause a headache. A more serious side effect is an allergic reaction, which requires immediate medical attention.

You can avoid most side effects by following the instructions from your doctor and pharmacist. Always inform your doctor of any allergies you have to medicines. Read the label on any kind of medicine you take.

The label on any kind of medicine explains when and how to use it as well as how much to use. Some medicines should not be taken together. In addition, some activities can be dangerous if you take certain medicines. For example, labels on medicines that cause sleepiness warn against operating machinery or driving. Ask your doctor or pharmacist if you do not understand a medicine label.

Drug Interactions

Taking two or more medicines at once can be dangerous. They may cause unexpected drug interactions. For example, one drug may become more effective or less effective, or the combination may produce different, more dangerous side effects that neither drug would have caused when taken by itself. Taking medicines with certain foods can also cause interaction problems. Always let your doctor and pharmacist know what other medicines you are taking before starting a new medicine.

> You can buy over-the-counter (OTC) medicines without a prescription. *Why is it important to carefully read the label on any medicine?*

Health SKILLS ACTIVITY

Decision Making

Scheduling a *Dosage*

Jason is on summer vacation. He gets sick, and his doctor prescribes medicine for him. The medication makes Jason feel sleepy and light-headed after he takes it. The label on the bottle warns patients not to use heavy machinery within four hours of taking the medicine. Jason is supposed to take it once a day, but he earns money by mowing lawns. Now Jason is worried about using the mower while he's on the medication.

Remember the six steps of the decision-making process:

1. State the situation.
2. List the options.
3. Weigh the possible outcomes.
4. Consider your values.
5. Make a decision and act on it.
6. Evaluate the decision.

What Would You Do? Apply the six steps above to help Jason make a healthful choice. What would you suggest that Jason do?

Tolerance

When someone uses a particular medicine for a long period of time, the person's body may develop a tolerance. Tolerance is *the body's need for larger and larger amounts of a drug to produce the same effect.* The concept of tolerance can apply to medicine as well as alcohol and other drugs. In some cases, tolerance may cause a medicine to lose its effectiveness over time.

The *more* an antibiotic is used, the **less effective** it becomes.

A person may go through withdrawal when he or she stops using the medicine. These symptoms will gradually ease over time. If you experience withdrawal after using a medicine, talk to your doctor. You may need to be prescribed a different medication. Symptoms of medicine withdrawal can include:

- Nervousness.
- Insomnia.
- Severe headaches.
- Vomiting.
- Chills.
- Cramps.

Antibiotic Resistance

The more an antibiotic is used, the less effective it becomes. This is especially true when an antibiotic is overused. Why? Antibiotics kill harmful illness-causing bacteria in the body. With frequent exposure, however, bacteria often build up a resistance to antibiotics. Bacteria adapt to, or overcome, the medicine. Bacteria can also develop a resistance when antibiotics are not taken as prescribed. For example, if the prescription label says to take the medicine for 14 days, and you stop after 7 days, the bacteria may still be in your body and could make you sick again. Medicines should always be used wisely, and they should be used only as directed.

>>> Reading Check

IDENTIFY *Name two risks of using medicines.* ■

The MRSA bacteria can infect a simple scrape and move to the lungs. Most antibiotics will not cure it. *Why might these bacteria be so resistant to antibiotics?*

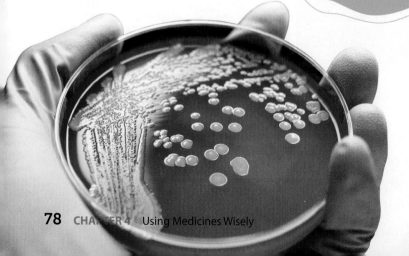

By R Parulan Jr./Flickr/Getty Images

LESSON 2

REVIEW

>>> After You Read

1. **VOCABULARY** Define the term *side effect.* Use it in an original sentence.
2. **DESCRIBE** What factors determine a medicine's effect on the body?
3. **LIST** Name two ways medicines are taken into the body.

>>> Thinking Critically

4. **ANALYZE** Why might a doctor prescribe different medicines for two people with the same illness?
5. **HYPOTHESIZE** Milla's doctor has prescribed a medicine to treat a case of poison ivy. She also regularly takes medicine because she has trouble concentrating. Should Milla tell her doctor what medicine she is already taking? Why or why not?

>>> Applying Health Skills

6. **ACCESSING INFORMATION** Go online to research a popular drug that you have seen advertisements for. What condition does the drug treat? What are its side effects?

Review

Audio

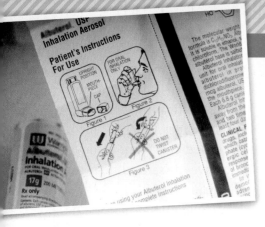

Using Medicines Correctly

BIG IDEA Using medicines improperly can cause harmful side effects.

Before You Read

QUICK WRITE Write a short paragraph about what you think might happen if a painkiller were used incorrectly.

▶ Video

As You Read

STUDY ORGANIZER Make the study organizer on page 89 to record the information presented in Lesson 3.

Vocabulary

› medicine misuse
› medicine abuse

🔊 Audio

🔤 Bilingual Glossary

Developing Good Character

Responsibility You can show responsibility by sharing information about the dangers of drug misuse with your family. Urge parents or guardians to throw away any medicines that have expired. *What are some other steps you can take to demonstrate responsibility at home?*

IMPROPER USE OF MEDICINES

MAIN IDEA Misusing medicines can be as harmful as using illegal drugs.

Medicines are types of drugs. Medicines are intended to be helpful, not harmful. They can prevent and cure diseases, fight germs, and relieve pain. If they are not used properly, however, medicines can be as harmful as illegal drugs. They can cause addiction, injury, and even death. If you use medicines improperly as a teen, it can result in serious health problems not only now but also later in life.

Both prescription medicines and over-the-counter medicines carry labels warning of possible side effects. Using too much medicine or using it too often can cause serious damage to body systems. For example, using too much of a medicine could cause liver or kidney failure. Certain medicines can also be very dangerous to unborn babies, newborns, or young children. A woman who is pregnant or plans to become pregnant should talk to a doctor before she takes any medicine.

Medicine Misuse

Medicines have many benefits when they are used correctly. Research studies show that most teens—96 percent—do use medicines correctly. *Taking medicine in a way that is not intended* is known as medicine misuse.

> If not used properly, *medicines* can be as **harmful** as *illegal drugs.*

Taking more medicine than a doctor instructs is one example of misusing medicines. Another example is failure to follow the directions on the label. Medicine misuse can be dangerous. It may only prevent you from getting the full benefits of a medicine. At worst, however, medicine misuse can seriously harm your health. This is why medicines need to be taken with great care.

⟩⟩⟩ Reading Check

RECALL *How can medicine misuse affect a person's health?*

Medicine Abuse

Medicine abuse is *intentionally using medicines in ways that are unhealthful and illegal.* Medicine abuse is a form of drug abuse. Some teens believe that prescription and OTC medicines are safer than illegal drugs. However, medicines are safe only if used properly. People may abuse medicines for several reasons:

- **To lose weight** A healthy diet and exercise are the safest way to maintain a healthy weight.
- **To stay awake** Getting plenty of sleep and learning strategies to manage your time wisely will help you study effectively.

- **To get "high"** A dangerous trend is the practice of having "pill parties," in which party-goers mix whatever OTC and prescription medicines may be available. Using medicine that is not prescribed for you is both illegal and dangerous and could even cause death.

Some medications have to be taken at certain times of the day. *How can you remember when to take a medication?*

Using a medicine prescribed to someone else is also medicine abuse. Medicines are prescribed for a specific person to treat a specific illness. Using someone else's medicine, even if you think you have the same illness, is both illegal and unsafe.

A danger of both medicine abuse and medicine misuse is the risk of overdose. An overdose is when someone takes too much medicine at once. Misusing medicines can also lead to addiction. The best way to make sure you are using a medicine safely is to follow the instructions on the label.

Health SKILLS ACTIVITY

Practicing Healthful Behaviors

Handling *Medicine* Safely in Your *Home*

What do you know about medicine safety in the home? Follow these guidelines to store, use, and dispose of medicine safely.

* Know what medicines are in your home and what they are used to treat.

* Store medicines in a cool, dry place.

* Keep medicines safely sealed in childproof containers, and keep them out of the reach of children.

* Never share prescription medicines. They could cause serious harm to someone else.

* Do not use OTC medicines for more than ten days at a time without first checking with your doctor.

* Before taking two or more medicines at the same time, get your doctor's approval. Combining medicines can cause harmful side effects.

* Do not use medicines that have passed their expiration date.

* To safely dispose of outdated or unused liquid or pills, flush them down the toilet.

On Your Own

Create a "Medicine Safety Checklist" that you can use at home. Review the completed checklist with your family. Post the list in an appropriate spot in your home.

HOW TO USE MEDICINES SAFELY

MAIN IDEA Medicines are helpful only when they are used properly.

When using medicines, it is important to keep them out of reach of young children. *Why is it important to be responsible when using medicines?*

Medicines can be helpful, but they can also cause serious harm. This is why they should be taken with great care. To avoid misuse, follow these guidelines:

- Follow the instructions on the label.
- Take the correct dosage for the recommended length of time. If you experience side effects from a prescription drug, contact your doctor before you stop using the medicine.
- Do not take medicines after their expiration date.
- Do not give prescription medicines to someone else. Do not use a medicine prescribed for an earlier illness without asking your doctor.

Never give **prescription** *medicines* to **someone** else.

- Contact your doctor if you do not understand the label instructions, if you experience any unusual or unpleasant side effects, or if you accidentally take too much medicine.
- Store all medicines safely—in a cool, dry place, in their original containers, and out of reach of children.

>>> Reading Check

GIVE EXAMPLES *What are three ways to use medicines safely?* ■

>>> After You Read

1. **VOCABULARY** Define the term *medicine misuse*. Use it in an original sentence.
2. **DESCRIBE** What are three ways you can avoid medicine abuse?
3. **COMPARE AND CONTRAST** How does medicine abuse differ from medicine misuse?

>>> Thinking Critically

4. **DISCUSS** How can taking medicines not prescribed for you, or mixing medicines, harm your health?
5. **EVALUATE** Tasha's friend has offered her some of her prescription medication. Tasha asks you whether she should take it. What advice would you give her and why?

>>> Applying Health Skills

6. **APPLY** Create a script for a commercial or PSA that explains how people can use their health care providers, pharmacists, and medicine labels to ensure that they are using their medicines properly.

Review

Audio

©Comstock/Alamy

Making Smart Choices *about* Medicines

WHAT YOU WILL NEED

* Three index cards per student
* One pencil or pen per student
* Internet or library access

WHAT YOU WILL DO

1 In teams of three, use each of your index cards to write one medicine you might find at a pharmacy. Each group should compile a total of nine different medications.

2 Research the health benefits and risks associated with each of the medicines you have listed. On the back of each card, list two benefits and two risks for each medication.

3 When you are finished, place all the completed cards face down in the middle of the table. Your teacher will then name a category, such as how the medicine enters the body, whether it is a prescription or OTC medicine, or which one carries the most risk.

4 For each round, your team will turn the cards over and sort them into the proper category. The winner is the team that completes the most rounds successfully.

A medicine can be either helpful or harmful to the body, depending on whether it is used properly and how it affects your body. Some medicines can protect you from certain diseases or are used to manage specific conditions. Others cure diseases, kill germs, relieve symptoms, or treat minor injuries. This activity will help you better understand the health risks and benefits of using different medications.

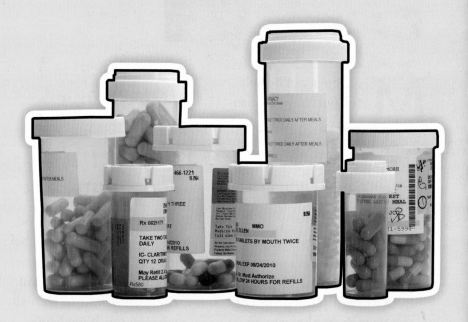

WRAPPING IT UP

Create a "How to Use Medicines Wisely" checklist that explains the steps to use when making a decision about using a medicine. Keep in mind the purpose of the medication, the way a medication affects your body, the health benefits and risks of a medication, and how the medication is used.

Jeffrey Coolidge/Getty Images

READING REVIEW

FOLDABLES and Other Study Aids

Take out the Foldable® that you created for Lesson 1 and any study organizers that you created for Lessons 2–3. Find a partner and quiz each other using these study aids.

LESSON 1 Types of Medicines

BIG IDEA Using medicines wisely is a sign of good personal and consumer health.

* A medicine is a drug that can prevent or cure an illness or ease its symptoms.
* Different medicines are used in various ways and serve different purposes in the body.
* Medicines in the United States are carefully controlled by the Food and Drug Administration (FDA), which sets standards for medicine safety and effectiveness.
* Some medicines require written permission from a doctor (prescription medicines).
* Other medicines are available without a prescription (over-the-counter [OTC] medicines).

LESSON 2 How Medicines Affect Your Body

BIG IDEA Medicines can contribute to good health when used properly.

* Different types of medicines can be used or taken in different ways.
* A medicine may be swallowed, injected, inhaled, or applied to the skin.
* Medicines affect different people in different ways and can be harmful if not used properly.

* Even proper use of medicines can result in sometimes dangerous side effects.
* The body can build up a tolerance to certain medicines over time, and frequent exposure to antibiotics may cause bacteria to build up a resistance.
* Always use medicines only as directed, and always read and follow all the instructions on the label.

LESSON 3 Using Medicines Correctly

BIG IDEA Using medicines improperly can cause harmful side effects.

* Misusing or abusing medicines can be as harmful as using illegal drugs.
* Taking medicine in a way that is not intended is medicine misuse.
* Medicine abuse is intentionally using medicines in ways that are unhealthful and illegal.
* Medicines are helpful only when they are used properly.
* Using medicines properly involves reading and following label instructions and taking the correct dosage for the recommended length of time.
* Always store medicines safely—in a cool, dry, secure place that is out of the reach of children.

 Review

 Web Quest

ASSESSMENT

Reviewing Vocabulary *and* Main Ideas

> over-the-counter (OTC) medicine
> resistance
> side effects
> prescription medicine
> tolerance
> medicine
> vaccine
> antibiotic

≫ On a sheet of paper, write the numbers 1–8. After each number, write the term from the list that best completes each statement.

LESSON 1 Types of Medicines

1. A(n) _____ is a medicine that can be sold only with a written order from a doctor.

2. A medicine that prevents a disease from developing is called a(n) _____.

3. A(n) _____ is a type of medicine that is used to treat a bacterial infection.

4. A drug that prevents or cures a disease or illness or eases its symptoms is called _____.

5. You can buy a(n) _____ without a written order from a doctor.

LESSON 2 How Medicines Affect Your Body

6. Drowsiness and nausea are examples of _____ that you could have from taking medicine.

7. Frequent exposure to antibiotics can cause bacteria to adapt to, or build up a _____ to, these drugs.

8. If you use a particular medicine for a long period of time, your body may develop a _____ for it.

≫ On a sheet of paper, write the numbers 9–14. Write *True* or *False* for each statement below. If the statement is false, change the underlined word or phrase to make it true.

LESSON 3 Using Medicines Correctly

9. Taking more of a medicine than a doctor instructs is an example of <u>medicine misuse</u>.

10. An important part of storing medicines safely is to keep them out of the reach of <u>adults</u>.

11. One way to make sure you are using a medicine safely is to <u>ignore</u> the instructions on the label.

12. <u>Only prescription medicines</u> carry labels warning of possible side effects.

13. A danger of both medicine abuse and medicine misuse is the risk of <u>drug overdose</u>.

14. It is <u>always</u> okay to share prescription medicines.

 eAssessment

🗣 *Thinking* **Critically**

15. PREDICT How could medicine misuse or abuse affect each side of your health triangle?

16. INTERPRET You have gotten sick, so your doctor has prescribed you some medicine. After taking the medicine, however, you break out in a rash. What should you do?

17. ANALYZE What can you do to help make sure you use a prescription medicine properly?

➤ *Write* **About It**

18. OPINION Write a blog post about the benefits and dangers of medicines. Explain ways that medicines can contribute to good health if used properly and ways they can be harmful if they are misused or abused.

19. DESCRIPTIVE WRITING Imagine that you have a medicine cabinet at home that is full of many different types of medicine. Explain how you would go about organizing the medicine cabinet to help make it safer for your family.

Ⓐ Ⓑ Ⓒ Ⓓ STANDARDIZED TEST PRACTICE

Writing

Read the prompts below. On a separate sheet of paper, write an essay that addresses each prompt. Use information from the chapter to support your writing. Refer to the tips in the right column.

1. Carl experiences back pain and visits his doctor, who prescribes a prescription painkiller. His friend Matt pulls a muscle playing basketball. Matt asks Carl if he can share his medicine. Explain why Carl should not share his prescription medicine with his friend Matt.

2. Imagine that you are a pharmacist working in a drugstore. A customer is confused by the label on the over-the-counter medicine. Write a dialogue in which you explain the different parts of a medicine label to ensure that they are using the medication properly.

Whenever you begin writing, first determine your task, audience, and purpose. Ask yourself the following questions: What is my topic? What are the guidelines of my essay? Is my purpose to explain a topic or persuade my audience? Who will be reading my writing? Understanding your task, audience, and purpose will help you accomplish your writing goal.

CHAPTER 1

Foldables®

Make this Foldable® to help you organize the facts about tobacco you learn in Lesson 1.

1 Begin with a plain sheet of notebook paper. Fold up the bottom edge to form a pocket. Glue the edges.

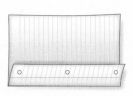

2 Fold the paper in half along the short axis to form a booklet.

3 Label the front of the booklet *Facts About Tobacco,* and label the inside pockets *What Is Tobacco?* and *Chemicals in Tobacco.* Place an index card or quarter sheet of notebook paper into each pocket.

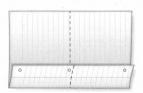

On index cards or quarter sheets of notebook paper, take notes on the different types of tobacco products and the harmful chemicals they contain. Store your notes in the appropriate pocket of your Foldable®.

Study Organizers

Use the following study organizers to record the information presented in Lessons 2–5.

Lesson 2:
Key Word Cluster

Lesson 3:
K-W-L Chart

K	W	L

Lesson 4:
Two-Column Chart

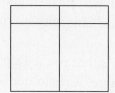

Lesson 5:
Index Cards

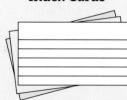

CHAPTER 2

Foldables®

Make this Foldable® to help you organize what you learn in Lesson 1 about alcohol use and teens.

1 Begin with a plain sheet of 11″ x 17″ paper. Fold the short sides inward so that they meet in the middle.

2 Fold the top to the bottom.

3 Unfold and cut along the inside fold lines to form four tabs.

4 Label the tabs *What Is Alcohol, Why Do Some Teens Use Alcohol, Reasons Not to Drink,* and *Consequences of Alcohol Use.*

Under the appropriate tab, record what you learn about these four topics.

Study Organizers

Use the following study organizers to record the information presented in Lessons 2–4.

Lesson 2:
Index Cards

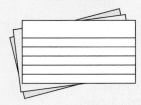

Lesson 3:
Outline

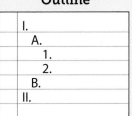

Lesson 4:
Key Word Cluster

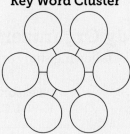

CHAPTER 3

Foldables®

Make this Foldable® to help you organize what you learn in Lesson 1 about drug use and abuse.

1 Begin with a plain sheet of notebook paper. Fold the sheet along the long axis, leaving a ½" tab along the side.

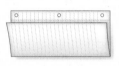

2 Fold the paper into thirds.

3 Unfold the paper and cut the shorter flap along both folds to create two tabs.

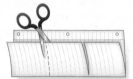

4 Label the long tab at the top *Drug Use and Abuse,* and label the three shorter tabs *Physical Consequences, Mental/Emotional Consequences,* and *Social Consequences.*

Under the appropriate tabs, record what you learn about the consequences of drug use and abuse.

Study Organizers

Use the following study organizers to record the information presented in Lessons 2–3.

Lesson 2:
K-W-L Chart

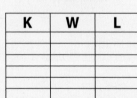

K	W	L

Lesson 3:
Key Word Cluster

CHAPTER 4

Foldables®

Make this Foldable® to help you organize what you learn in Lesson 1 about types of medicines.

1 Begin with a plain sheet of notebook paper. Fold the sheet of paper along the long axis, leaving a 1/2" tab along the side.

2 Fold the paper in half, and then fold it in half again.

3 Unfold the paper and cut the top layer along the three fold lines. This makes four tabs.

4 Turn the paper vertically, and label the four tabs *What Are Medicines, The Purpose of Medicines, Prescription Medicines,* and *Non-Prescription Medicines.*

Under the appropriate tab, record what you learn about the types and purposes of medicines.

Study Organizers

Use the following study organizers to record the information presented in Lessons 2–3.

Lesson 2:
Two-Column Chart

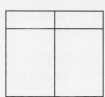

Lesson 3:
Venn Diagram

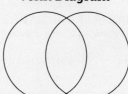

Glossary/Glosario

English

A

Abstinence (AB stuh nuhns) The conscious, active choice not to participate in high-risk behaviors.

Addiction A mental or physical need for a drug or other substance.

Addictive Capable of causing a user to develop intense cravings.

Advocacy Taking action in support of a cause.

Alcohol (AL kuh hawl) A drug created by a chemical reaction in some foods, especially fruits and grains.

Alcohol abuse Using alcohol in ways that are unhealthy, illegal, or both.

Alcohol poisoning A dangerous condition that results when a person drinks excessive amounts of alcohol over a short time period.

Alcoholism A disease in which a person has a physical and psychological need for alcohol.

Alternative (ahl TER nuh tihv) Another way of thinking or acting.

Alveoli (al VEE oh lye) The tiny air sacs in the lungs.

Anabolic steroids (a nuh BAH lik STAIR oydz) Substances that cause muscle tissue to develop at an abnormally high rate.

Antibiotics (an ti by AH tiks) Medicines that reduce or kill harmful bacteria in the body.

Attitude (AT ih tood) Feelings and beliefs.

B

Binge drinking Having several drinks in a short period of time.

Blood alcohol concentration (BAC) The amount of alcohol in the blood.

Bronchi (BRAHNG ky) Two passageways that branch from the trachea, one to each lung.

C

Carbon monoxide (KAR buhn muh NAHK syd) A colorless, odorless, poisonous gas produced when tobacco burns.

Cirrhosis (suh ROH suhs) The scarring and destruction of liver tissue.

Club drugs Illegal drugs that are found mostly in nightclubs or at all-night dance parties called raves.

Cold turkey Stopping all use of tobacco products immediately.

Communication The exchange of information through the use of words or actions.

Español

abstinencia Opción activa y conciente de no participar en comportamientos de alto riesgo.

adicción Necesidad mental o física de una droga u otra substancia.

adictivo Capaz de ocasionar que el consumidor desarrolle una necesidad repentina intensa.

promoción Actuar en apoyo de una causa.

alcohol Droga producida por una reacción química en algunos alimentos, especialmente frutas y granos.

abuso de alcohol Uso de alcohol en formas que son no saludables, ilegales, o ambas.

intoxicación con alcohol Condición peligrosa que ocurre cuando una persona consume cantidades de alcohol excesivas en un corto periodo de tiempo.

alcoholismo Enfermedad que se caracteriza por la necesidad física y psicológica de consumir alcohol.

alternativa Otra forma de pensar o actuar.

alveolos Pequeños sacos de aire en los pulmones.

esteroides anabólicos Sustancias que causan que los tejidos musculares se desarrollen rápida y anormalmente.

antibióticos Medicinas que disminuyen o matan bacterias dañinas en el cuerpo.

actitud Sentimientos y creencias.

borrachera Ingerir varias bebidas en un periodo de tiempo corto.

concentración de alcohol en la sangre Cantidad de alcohol en la sangre.

bronquios Dos pasajes que se ramifican desde la tráquea hacia los dos pulmones.

monóxido de carbono Gas incoloro, inodoro y tóxico que produce el tabaco al quemarse.

cirrosis Cicatrización y destrucción del tejido del hígado.

drogas de clubs Drogas ilegales que normalmente son utilizadas en discotecas y otras fiestas que duran toda la noche llamadas raves.

parar en seco Acto de parar inmediatamente el uso de productos que contienen tabaco inmediatamente.

comunicación Intercambio de información a través del uso de palabras y acciones.

English

Español

Conflict resolution A life skill that involves solving a disagreement in a way that satisfies both sides.

resolución de un conflicto Habilidad que implica el hecho de resolver un desacuerdo satisfaciendo a los dos lados.

Cultural background The beliefs, customs, and traditions of a specific group of people.

base cultural Creencias, costumbres y tradiciones de un grupo especifico de personas.

Culture the collected beliefs, customs, and behaviors of a group

cultura Colección de creencias, costumbres y comportamientos de un grupo.

Cumulative (KYOO myuh luh tiv) risk When one risk factor adds to another to increase danger.

riesgo acumulativo Cuando un factor riesgoso se suma a otro e incrementa el peligro.

D

Decision making The process of making a choice or solving a problem.

tomar decisiones Proceso de hacer una selección o de resolver un problema.

Depressant (di PRE suhnt) A drug that slows down the body's functions and reactions, including heart and breathing rates.

sedante Droga que disminuye las funciones y reacciones del cuerpo, incluso el ritmo cardiaco y la respiración.

Detoxification (dee tahk si fi KAY shuhn) The physical process of freeing the body of an addictive substance.

desintoxicación Proceso físico de liberar al cuerpo de una sustancia adictiva.

Drug A substance other than food that changes the structure or function of the body or mind.

droga Sustancia no alimenticia que causa cambios en la estructura o el funcionamiento del cuerpo o la mente.

Drug abuse Intentionally using drugs in a way that is unhealthful or illegal.

abuso de drogas Uso de drogas intencionalmente en una forma no saludable o ilegal.

Drug misuse Taking or using medicine in a way that is not intended.

mal empleo de drogas Tomar o usar medicina de una forma que no es la indicada.

Drug rehabilitation a process where the person relearns how to live without the abused drug

rehabilitacion de las drogas Proceso por el cual una persona vuelve a aprender como vivir sin el abuso de una droga.

E

Emphysema (em fuh SEE muh) A disease that results in the destruction of the alveoli in the lungs.

enfisema Enfermedad que resulta de la destrucción de los alvéolos en los pulmones.

Enablers Persons who create an atmosphere in which the alcoholic can comfortably continue his or her unacceptable behavior.

habilitadores Personas que crean una atmósfera en la cual el alcohólico puede continuar su comportamiento inaceptable de una forma cómoda.

Environment (en VY ruhn muhnt) All the living and nonliving things around you.

medio Todas las cosas vivas y no vivas que te rodean.

F

Fatty liver A condition in which fats build up in the liver and cannot be broken down.

higado adiposo Condición en la cual la grasa se forma en el hígado y no puede ser deshecha.

Fetal (FEE tuhl) alcohol syndrome (FAS) A group of alcohol-related birth defects that include both physical and mental problems.

síndrome de alcoholismo fetal Conjunto de defectos de nacimiento causados por el alcohol que incluyen problemas físicos y mentales.

G

Goal setting The process of working toward something you want to accomplish.

establecer metas Proceso de esforzarte para lograr algo que quieres.

Glossary/Glosario

English

Español

Hallucinogens (huh LOO suhn uh jenz) Drugs that distort moods, thoughts, and senses.

alucinógeno Droga que altera el estado de ánimo, los pensamientos y los sentidos.

Health The combination of physical, mental/emotional, and social well-being.

salud Combinación de bienestar físico, mental/emocional y social.

Health care system All the medical care available to a nation's people, the way they receive the care, and the way the care is paid for.

sistema de cuidado de la salud Servicios médicos disponibles para a la gente de una nación y las formas en las cuales estos son pagados.

Health insurance A plan in which a person pays a set fee to an insurance company in return for the company's agreement to pay some or all medical expenses when needed.

seguro médico Plan en el que una persona paga una cantidad fija a una compañía de seguros que acuerda cubrir parte o la totalidad de los gastos médicos.

Health skills skills that help you become and stay healthy

habilidades de salud Habilidades que ayudan a ser y mantenerte saludable.

Heredity (huh RED I tee) The passing of traits from parents to their biological children.

herencia Transferencia de características de los padres biológicos a sus hijos.

Inhalants (in HAY luhntz) The vapors of chemicals that are sniffed or inhaled to get a "high."

inhalantes Los vapores de substancias químicas que son olidos o inhalados para drogarse.

Inhibition A conscious or unconscious restraint on his or her behaviors or actions.

inhibición Reprimir comportamientos o acciones consiente o inconscientemente.

Intervention A gathering in which family and friends get the problem drinker to agree to seek help.

intervención Reunión en la cual familia y amigos hacen que la persona con problemas alcohólicos busque ayuda.

Intoxicated (in TAHK suh kay tuhd) Being drunk.

intoxicado(a) Estar borracho.

Lifestyle factors Behaviors and habits that help determine a person's level of health.

factores del estilo de vida Conductas y hábitos que ayudan a determinar el nivel de salud de una persona.

Long-term goal A goal that you plan to reach over an extended period of time.

meta a largo plazo Objetivo que planeas alcanzar en un largo periodo de tiempo.

Mainstream smoke The smoke that is inhaled and then exhaled by a smoker.

humo directo Humo que el fumador aspira y exhala.

Malnutrition A condition in which the body doesn't get the nutrients it needs to grow and function properly.

desnutrición Cual es una afección en la que el cuerpo no recibe los nutrientes que necesita para crecer y funcionar de forma adecuada.

Managed care A health insurance plan that saves money by encouraging patients and providers to select lest costly forms of care.

cuidado controlado Plan de seguro médico que ahorra dinero al limitar la selección de doctores de las personas.

Marijuana Dried leaves and flowers of the hemp plant, called cannabis sativa.

mariguana Hojas y flores secas de la planta de cáñamo, llamada cannabis sativa.

Media Various methods for communicating information.

medios de difusión Diversos métodos de comunicar información.

Media literacy The ability to understand the goals of advertising and the media.

conocimiento de los medios de comunicación Habilidad de entender las metas de la publicidad en los medios publicitarios.

English

Español

Medicine A drug that prevents or cures an illness or eases its symptoms.

medicina Droga que previene o cura enfermedades o que alivia sus síntomas.

Medicine abuse Intentionally using medicines in ways that are unhealthful and illegal.

medicina abuso Intencionalmente el uso de medicamentos en formas que son insalubres e ilegales.

Medicine misuse Taking medicine in a way that is not intended.

el abuso de medicamentos Tomar un medicamento de una manera que no es la intención.

Mind-body connection How your emotions affect your physical and overall health and how your overall health affects your emotions.

conexión de la mente con el cuerpo Forma en la cual tus emociones afectan tu salud física y general, y como tu salud general afecta tus emociones.

Minor A person under the age of adult rights and responsibilities.

menor Persona que es menor de en que se tienen la edad de derechos y responsabilidades de adultos.

Narcotics (nar KAH tics) Drugs that get rid of pain and dull the senses.

narcótico Droga que alivia el dolor y entorpece los sentidos.

Nicotine (NIH kuh teen) An addictive, or habit-forming, drug found in tobacco.

nicotina Droga adictiva, que forma hábito, encontrada en el tabaco.

Nicotine replacement therapies (NRT) Products that assist a person in breaking a tobacco habit.

terapias para remplazar la nicotina Productos que ayudan a las personas a romper el hábito del tabaco.

Over-the-counter (OTC) medicine A medicine that you can buy without a doctor's permission.

medicina sin receta Medicina que se puede comprar sin receta de un médico.

Passive smoker A nonsmoker who breathes in secondhand smoke.

fumador pasivo Persona que no fuma pero que inhala humo secundario.

Peers People close to you in age who are a lot like you.

compañeros Personas de tu grupo de edad que se parecen a ti de muchas maneras.

Physical dependence An addiction in which the body develops a chemical need for a drug.

dependencia física Adicción por la cual el cuerpo llega a tener una necesidad química de una droga.

Point of sale promotion Advertising campaigns in which a product is promoted at a store's checkout counter.

punto de promoción de venta Campañas de publicidad en las cuales un producto puede adquirirse en la caja.

Prescription (prih SKRIP shuhn) medicine A medicine that can be obtained legally only with a doctor's written permission.

medicinas bajo receta Medicina que puede ser obtenida legalmente solo con el permiso escrito de un doctor.

Prevention Taking steps to avoid something.

prevención Tomar pasos para evitar algo.

Preventive care Steps taken to keep disease or injury from happening or getting worse.

cuidado preventivo Medidas que se toman para evitar que ocurran enfermedades o daños o que empeoren.

Primary care provider Health care professional who provides checkups and general care.

profesional médico principal Profesional de la salud que proporciona exámenes médicos y cuidado general.

Product placement A paid arrangement a company has made to show its products in media such as television or film.

colocación de un producto Acuerdo pagado hecho por una compañía para mostrar su producto en los medios de publicidad.

Psychological dependence A person's belief that he or she needs a drug to feel good or function normally.

dependencia psicológica Cuando una persona cree que necesita una droga para sentirse bien o para trabajar normalmente.

Glossary/Glosario

English	Español

Reaction time The ability of the body to respond quickly and appropriately to situations.

Recovery The process of learning to live an alcohol-free life.

Refusal skills Strategies that help you say no effectively.

Relapse A return to the use of a drug after attempting to stop.

Reliable Trustworthy and dependable.

Risk The chance that something harmful may happen to your health and wellness.

Risk behavior An action or behavior that might cause injury or harm to you or others.

tiempo de reacción Habilidad del cuerpo de responder rápida y apropiadamente a diferentes situaciones.

recuperación Proceso de aprender a vivir una vida libre de alcohol.

habilidades de rechazo Estrategias que ayudan a decir no efectivamente.

recaída Regresar al uso de la droga después de haber intentado parar.

confiable Confiable y seguro.

riesgo Posibilidad de que algo dañino pueda ocurrir en tu salud y bienestar.

conducta arriesgada Acto o conducta que puede causarte daño o perjudicarte a ti o a otros.

Secondhand smoke Air that has been contaminated by tobacco smoke.

Short-term goal A goal that you can achieve in a short length of time.

Side effect A reaction to a medicine other than the one intended.

Sidestream smoke Smoke that comes from the burning end of a cigarette, pipe, or cigar.

Smokeless tobacco Ground tobacco that is chewed or inhaled through the nose.

Snuff finely ground tobacco that is inhaled or held in the mouth or cheeks

Specialist (SPEH shuh list) Health care professional trained to treat a special category of patients or specific health problems.

Stimulant (STIM yuh luhnt) A drug that speeds up the body's functions.

Stress The body's response to real or imagined dangers or other life events.

Substance abuse using illegal or harmful drugs, including any use of alcohol while under the legal drinking age

humo secundario Aire que está contaminado por el humo del tabaco.

meta a corto plazo Meta que uno puede alcanzar dentro de un breve periodo de tiempo.

efecto colateral Reacción inesperada de una medicina.

humo indirecto Humo que procede de un cigarrillo, pipa o cigarro encendido.

rapé Tabaco molido que es masticado o inhalado a través de la nariz.

rapé Tabaco molido finamente que es inhalado o mantenido en la boca o las mejillas.

especialista Profesional del cuidado de la salud que está capacitado para tratar una categoría especial de pacientes o un problema de salud específico.

estimulante Droga que acelera las funciones del cuerpo.

estrés Reacción del cuerpo hacia peligros reales o imaginarios u otros eventos en la vida.

abuso de sustancias Consumo de drogas ilegales o nocivas, incluso el consumo del alcohol en cualquiera de sus formas antes de la edad legal para beber.

English

T

Tar A thick, dark liquid that forms when tobacco burns.

Target audience A group of people for which a product is intended.

Tolerance (TAHL er ence) The body's need for larger and larger amounts of a drug to produce the same effect.

U

Ulcer (UHL ser) An open sore in the stomach lining.

V

Vaccine (vak SEEN) A preparation of dead or weakened pathogens that is introduced into the body to cause an immune response.

Values The beliefs that guide the way a person lives.

W

Wellness A state of well-being or balanced health over a long period of time.

Withdrawal A series of painful physical and mental symptoms that a person experiences when he or she stops using an addictive substance.

Español

alquitrán Líquido espeso y oscuro que forma el tabaco al quemarse.

publico objetivo Grupo de gente al cual es dirigido un producto específico.

tolerancia Necesidad del cuerpo de mayores cantidades de una droga para obtener el mismo efecto.

Úlcera Llaga abierta en el forro del estómago

vacuna Fórmula compuesta por gérmenes patógenos muertos o debilitados que es introducida en el cuerpo para causar una reacción inmune.

valores Creencias que guían la forma en la cual vive una persona.

bienestar Mantener una salud balanceada por un largo período de tiempo.

síndrome de abstinencia Series de síntomas físicos y mentales dolorosos por los cuales una persona pasa cuando para el uso de una sustancia adictiva.

Index

Index

Index

Interval Training

Getting fit takes time. One method, interval training, can show improvement in two weeks or less. Interval training consists of a mix of activities. First you do a few minutes of intense exercise. Next, you do easier, less-intense activity that enables your body to recover. Interval training can improve your cardiovascular endurance. It also helps develop speed and quickness.

Intervals are typically done as part of a running program. Not everyone wants to be a runner though. Intervals can also be done riding a bicycle or while swimming. On a bicycle, alternate fast pedaling with easier riding. In a pool, swim two fast laps followed by slower, easier laps.

What Will I Need?

» A running track or other flat area with marked distances like a football or soccer field.

» If at a park, 5–8 cones or flags to mark off distances of 30 to 100 yards.

» A training partner to help you push yourself (optional).

How Do I Start?

» After warming up, alternate brisk walking (or easy jogging). On a football field or track, walk 30 yards, jog 30 yards, and then run at a fast pace for 30 yards. Rest for one minute and repeat this circuit several times. If at a park, use cones or flags to mark off similar distances.

» Accelerate gradually into the faster strides so you stay loose and feel in control of the pace.

» If possible, alternate running up stadium steps instead of fast running on a track. This will help your coordination as well as your speed. Running uphill in a park would have similar benefits.

How Can I Stay Safe?

» Interval training works the heart and lungs. For this reason, a workout using interval training should be done only once or twice a week with a day off between workouts.

» Check with your doctor first. If you have any medical condition like high blood pressure or asthma, ask your doctor if interval training is safe for you.

FLIP 4 FITNESS

Flip for Fitness is for everyone. Non-athletes who avoid joining organized sports can develop a personal fitness plan to stay in shape. Even athletes can use some of the tips to cross train for their favorite sport.

Planning a Routine

Flip for Fitness helps you plan a fitness routine that helps your body slowly adjust to activity. Over time, you will increase both the length of time you spend and the number of times that you are physically active each week. Teens should aim to get at least one hour of physical activity each day. These periods of physical activity can be divided into shorter segments, such as three 20 minute segments each day. Exercise includes any physical activity, such as completing a fitness plan, playing individual or group sports, or even helping clean at home. The key is to keep your body moving.

Before You Start Exercising

Every activity session should begin with a warm-up to prepare your body for exercise. Warm-ups raise your body temperature and get your muscles ready for physical activity. Easy warm-up activities include walking, marching, and jogging, as well as basic calisthenics or stretches. As you increase the time you spend doing a fitness activity, you should increase the time you spend warming up. Check the Sample Physical Fitness Plan in Teen Health in Connect Ed.

Fitness Information *and* Resources

Fitness Apps *and* Other Resources

» **USDA's MyPlate** The MyPlate Super Tracker is a free online fitness and diet tracker. To review the tracker, go online to https://www.choosemyplate.gov and search for "Super Tracker".

» Additionally, organizations such as the **American Heart Association** and **KidsHealth** provide resources on developing walking programs. The online addresses are: http://startwalkingnow.org and http://kidshealth.org.

» Finally, smartphone and tablet users can download several nutrition and fitness tracking apps. Many are free of charge. Use the terms "fitness", "exercise", or "workout" when searching for apps.

Accessing Information

» The *Teen Health* online program includes resources to develop your own fitness plan. Check out the **Fitness Zone** resources in ConnectEd.

» The Centers for Disease Control and Prevention's, **Body & Mind (BAM)** web site also provide fitness information. The online address is: http://www.bam.gov. Search for "physical activity" or "activity cards."

Safety Tips

On the following pages, you'll find fitness activities for groups or individuals. Each activity includes information on what you'll need, how to start, and how to stay safe. Safety is the most important factor.

⚠ Always be aware of where you are and don't take any unnecessary chances.

⚠ Obey the rules of the road while riding your bicycle, avoid unsafe areas, and use the proper safety equipment when working out.

⚠ Finally, remember to drink water and to rest between exercise sessions.

5 Elements *of* Fitness

When developing a fitness plan, it's helpful to have a goal. Maybe your goal is to comfortably ride your bike to school each day or maybe you want to complete the Tour de France in the future. Regardless of the reasons why you develop a fitness plan, focusing on the five elements of fitness will help you achieve overall physical fitness. The five elements are:

1 Cardiovascular Endurance

The ability of the heart and lungs to function efficiently over time without getting tired. Familiar examples are jogging, walking, bike riding, and swimming.

2 Muscle Endurance

The ability of a muscle or a group of muscles to work non-stop without getting tired. Many activities that build cardiovascular endurance also build muscular endurance, such as jogging, walking, and bike riding.

3 Muscle Strength

The ability of the muscle to produce force during an activity. Activities that can help build muscle strength include push-ups, pull-ups, lifting weights, and running stairs.

4 Flexibility

The ability to move a body part freely, without pain. Improve your flexibility by stretching gently before and after exercise.

5 Body Composition

The amount of body fat a person has compared with the amount of lean mass, which is bone, muscle, and fluid. A healthy body is made up of more lean mass and less body fat. Body composition is a result of diet, exercise, and heredity.

Fitness Circuit

Are you looking for a quick workout that will develop endurance, strength, and flexibility? A Fitness Circuit may be just what you need. Many public parks have Fitness Circuits (sometimes called Par Courses) with exercise stations located throughout a park. You walk or run between stations as part of your workout. A fitness circuit can also be created in your backyard or even a basement.

What Will I Need?

» Access to a public park or a home-made Fitness Circuit course.

» Comfortable workout clothes that wick away perspiration.

» Athletic shoes.

» Stopwatch (optional).

» Jump rope, dumbbells, exercise bands, or check out the Fitness Zone Clipboard Energizer Activity Cards, Circuit Training for ideas.

How Do I Start?

» In the park, read the instructions at each exercise station and perform the exercises as shown. Use the correct form. Try to do as many repetitions as you can for 30 seconds.

» After you finish the exercise, walk or run to the next station and complete that exercise.

» Check your heart rate to see how intensely you exercised at the end of the Fitness Circuit.

» Every month or so, consider adding a new exercise.

How Can I Stay Safe?

» Be alert to your surroundings in a public park. It is best to have a friend with you. It's also more fun to exercise with a friend.

» At home, leave enough room between stations to allow you to move and exercise freely. Avoid clutter in your exercise area.

» Perform the exercises correctly and at your own pace.

Walking

Walking is more than just a way to get from one place to another. It's also a great physical activity. By walking for as little as 30 minutes each day you can reduce your risk of heart disease, manage your weight, and even reduce stress. Walking requires very little equipment and you can do it almost anywhere. More good news: Walking is also something you can do by yourself or with friends and family.

Colin Hawkins/Cultura/Getty Images

What Will I Need?

» Running or walking shoes. Many athletic shoe stores sell both.

» Loose comfortable clothes that wick away perspiration. Layering is also a good idea. Consider adding a hat, sunglasses, and sunscreen if needed.

» Stopwatch and water bottle unless there are water fountains on your route.

» A pedometer or GPS to track your distance.

How Do I Start?

» Five minutes of easy stretching.

» Walk upright with good posture. Do not exaggerate your stride or swing your arms across your body.

» Build your time and distance slowly. One mile or 20 minutes every other day may be enough for the first couple weeks. Eventually you will want to walk at least 30-60 minutes five days a week.

How Can I Stay Safe?

» Let your parents know where you will be walking and how long you will be gone.

» Avoid wearing headphones if by yourself or if walking on a road or street.

Running *or* Jogging

Running or jogging is one of the best all-around fitness activities. Running uses the large muscles of the legs thereby burning lots of calories and also gives your heart and lungs a good workout in a shorter amount of time. Running also helps get you into condition to play team sports like basketball, football, or soccer. More good news is that running can be done on your schedule although it's also fun to run with a friend or two.

What Will I Need?

» A good pair of running shoes. Ask your Physical Education teacher or an employee at a specialist running shop to help you choose the right pair.

» Socks made of cotton or another type of material that wicks away perspiration.

» Bright colored or reflective clothing and shoes.

» A stopwatch or watch with a second sweep to time your runs or track your distance.

» Optional equipment might include a jacket or other layer depending on the weather, sunscreen, and sunglasses.

How Do I Start?

Your ultimate goal is to run at least 20 to 30 minutes at least 3 days a week. Use the training schedule shown below. Start by walking and gradually increasing the amount of time you run during each exercise session. Starting slowly will help your muscles and tendons adjust to the increased work load. Try spacing the three runs over an entire week so that you have one day in-between runs to recover.

How Can I Stay Safe?

» Use the correct equipment for the sport you have chosen.

» Running on a track, treadmill, or in a park with level ground will help you avoid foot or ankle injuries.

» Avoid running on the road, especially at night.

» Avoid wearing headphones unless you are on a track, treadmill, or another safe place. Safety experts agree that headphones can distract you from being alert to your surroundings.

Here is a plan to get you started as a runner:

» Start each run with a brisk 3-5 minute walk to warm-up.

» Take some time to slowly stretch the muscles and areas of the body involved in running. Avoid "bouncing" when stretching or trying to force a muscle or tendon to stretch when you start to feel tightness.

» Begin slowly and gradually increase your distance and speed. A good plan for the first several weeks is to alternate walking with easy running. The running plan included in this section can give you some tips on how to train for a 5K run.

» Use the "talk test." Can you talk in complete sentences during your training runs? If not, you are running too fast.

Training Schedule

M W F	Split Schedule	Duration
Week 1	Brisk 5 min. walk Walk: 60 - 90 seconds Run: 60 seconds	Repeat for 20 min.
Week 2 and 3	Brisk 5 min. walk Walk: 60 seconds Run: 60 - 90 seconds	Repeat for 20 min.
Week 4	Brisk 5 min. walk Walk: 60 seconds Run: 3 - 5 minutes	Repeat for 20 min.
Week 5+	Brisk 5 min. walk Run: 20 to 30 minutes	

Preparing *for* Sports *and* Other Activities

Do you want to play a sport? If so, think about developing a fitness plan for that sport. Some of the questions to ask yourself are: Does the sport require anaerobic activity, like running and jumping hurdles? Does the sport require aerobic fitness, like cross-country running? Other sports, such as football and track require muscular strength. Sports like basketball require special skills like dribbling, passing, and shot making. A workout plan for that sport will help you get into shape before organized practice and competition begins.

What Will I Need?

Each sport has different equipment requirements. Talk to a coach or physical education teacher about how to get ready for your sport. You can also conduct online research to learn what type of equipment you will need, such as:

» Proper footwear and workout clothes for a specific sport.

» What facilities are available for training and practice, such as a running track, tennis court, football or soccer field, or other safe open area.

» Where you can access weights and others form of resistance training as part of your training.

How Do I Start?

Now that your research is done, you can create your fitness plan. Include the type of exercises you will do each training day.

» Include a warm-up in your plan.

» List the duration of time that you will work out.

» Plan to exercise 3–5 days a week doing at least one kind of exercise each day. Remember to include stretching before every workout.

How Can I Stay Safe?

» Get instruction on how to use free weights and machines

» Make sure you start every activity with a warm-up.

» Ease into your fitness plan gradually so you do not pull a muscle or do too much too soon.

» Practice good nutrition and drink plenty of water to stay hydrated.